THE
PALMISTRY
WORKBOOK

The Art of Psychological Hand Analysis

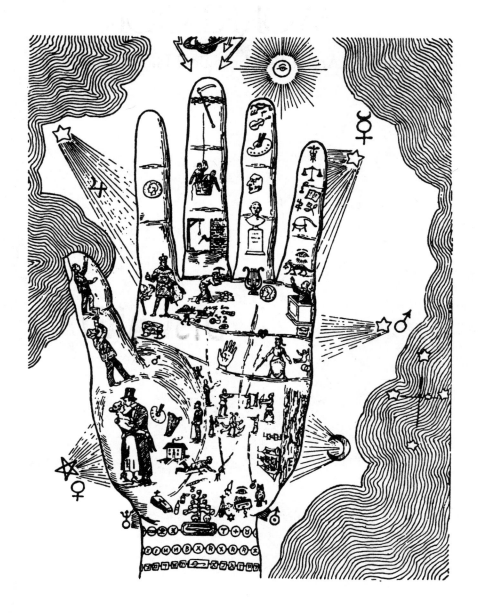

Frontispiece:
The Hand and Planetary Influences from *Die Wissenshaftliche Handlesekunst Chirosophie*, by Ernest Issberner-Haldane (Berlin, 1922). (Reprinted permission of Editorial Kier, Buenos Aires © 1966).

THE
PALMISTRY
WORKBOOK

NATHANIEL ALTMAN

Illustrated by Linda James

Sterling Publishing Co., Inc.   New York

7 9 10 8 6

Published in 1990 by Sterling Publishing Company, Inc.
387 Park Avenue South, New York, N.Y. 10016
Originally published in Great Britain by The Aquarian Press
© 1984 by Nathaniel Altman
Distributed in Canada by Sterling Publishing
% Canadian Manda Group, P. O. Box 920, Station U
Toronto, Ontario, Canada M8Z 5P9
Manufactured in the United States of America
All rights reserved

ISBN 0-85030-352-4

This book is dedicated to
Teresa Gómez de Barberi
with gratitude.

ACKNOWLEDGEMENTS

The author wishes to thank the following people who helped in the preparation of this book: José Alberto Rosa, MD, Gloria A. Lanza, Sadie Altman, Robert K. Altman, Wayne Perez.

CONTENTS

PREFACE

Like astrology, the ancient art and science of hand analysis has enjoyed increasing popularity in recent years. Although still tainted by images of gypsy fortune-tellers, a growing number of medical doctors, therapists, scientists and other serious individuals have discovered that the shape, contours and lines of the human hand are reliable indicators of character traits, health, intelligence and creative ability.

I first became interested in hand analysis while studying political science in South America. A friend was going to visit her cousin — who read hands — and invited me to join her. During the visit, her cousin read my hands, and I was deeply impressed by her insight and accuracy. After the analysis, she mentioned that I might also become a good hand reader if I wanted to invest the time and effort. She recommended several books for me to read and offered to give me some basic instruction before I returned to the United States. By the time I left South America, I had read the hands of over a hundred people, and began to collect hand prints to observe if any changes would occur in the hands in time.

Over the years my fascination with hands continued to grow. Although I had always been amazed at the ability of the hands to reveal past and potential illnesses, traumas and achievements, I became primarily interested in the psychological aspects of hand analysis. I was particularly impressed by the fact that in one minute the hands can sometimes reveal certain personality traits that could take a traditional psychologist months to uncover.

Although there are perhaps five or six popular books on palmistry available today, none are primarily devoted to the psychological dynamics of hand analysis. In addition, none of them deal specifically with life's major concerns — like sexuality, career, relationships and spirituality — in a comprehensive and unified way. I have long felt the need for a book that would not only discuss the various lines, mounts and other hand characteristics by themselves, but would provide an integrated study of hand characteristics as they relate specifically to these key areas of human interest and concern.

The Palmistry Workbook is that kind of book. The product of fifteen years of research and experience, it has been written with the ongoing guidance of a leading psychotherapist. Although the book will appeal to members of the helping professions — including physicians, therapists and social workers — it has been written primarily for the general reader and the serious palmistry student who wants to deepen his or her knowledge and expertise.

Good reading to you.

Nathaniel Altman
New York City, October 1983

Section I:
Grounding

Chapter 1

YOUR HAND: THE LIVING COMPUTER

The human hand created our entire civilization and culture. It has insured our survival through the years by fashioning implements for hunting and farming. It has created every tool from a simple hammer to the most sophisticated digital computer. With the aid of the hand, great ideas have been recorded which would otherwise have been lost to posterity. The exploration of outer space, as well as discoveries in microbiology, would not have been at all possible without the development of the hand-polished lens.

Through the harmonious co-operation of twenty-seven bones, dozens of muscles and millions of nerves, the human hand is a marvel of design and operation. It can grasp hundreds of pounds, and — in the case of karate masters — can smash bricks and break a table in two. Yet the hand can perform the most delicate brain surgery, is capable of creating the finest needlepoint design, or can play up to 960 notes per minute on a concert piano. Our hands express our love, our needs, and our desire to communicate. From the first months of life, our hands are our basic link to the world and help us learn and experience life.

The hand has fascinated us for thousands of years. Studies of the human hand — both as a tool for creative expression and as a mirror of our inner selves — go back over five thousand years. It is believed that the ancient Chinese began studying the hand as early as 3000 BC. In India at the same time, Aryan sages developed the study of hand analysis, *Hast Samudrika Shastra*, as part of a larger science (Samudrika Shastra), which interprets and forecasts human nature and destiny by scrutinizing the forehead, face, hands, chest and feet. Writings related to the study of the human hand can be found in Indian literature dating back to 2000 BC, while the earliest references to palmistry itself can be found in the Vedic text, *The Laws of Manu* (vi:50).

Although no written records remain, it is known that the ancient Chaldeans, Tibetans, Sumerians and Babylonians studied the science of hand analysis, as well as the early Hebrews, Egyptians and Persians. Throughout the Middle East today, hand reading, known as *Ilm-ul-kaff*, is a highly respected study and avocation.

The Greeks were enthusiastic students of hand symbology and hand analysis, and coined the term *chirosophy* (from *xier*, hand and *sophia*,

Figure 1.1: The open hand, with notes relating to palmistry. From a manuscript in French square and rabbinic writing of the late thirteenth century. (Reprinted courtesy of the British Library, London.)

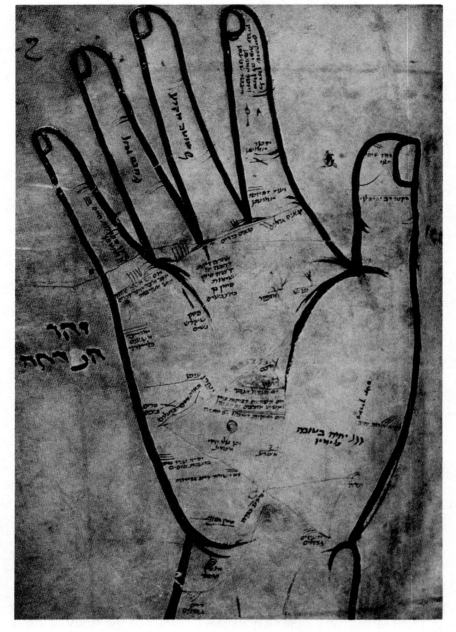

Figure 1.2: From Aristotle: *Chiromantia* (Ulm, 1490). (Reprinted courtesy of The New York Public Library.)

wisdom). Aristotle was supposed to have found an ancient Arabic document on chirosophy on an altar to Hermes. He is credited with having authored several specialized treatises on hands, including one written especially for Alexander the Great. He was particularly interested in the markings of the hand, and the significance they have in our lives:

> The lines are not written into the human hands without reason, they come from heavenly influences and man's own individuality.
>
> *De coelo et mundi causa*

His book *Chiromantia* — from which Figure 1.2 was taken — is considered among the earliest surviving texts on the subject of scientific hand analysis.

In addition to Alexander the Great, Claudius Galen, Anaxagoras,

Hippocrates, Artemodoros of Ephesus and Claudius Ptolemaeus were serious students of medical and psychological chirosophy as well as *chiromancy*, the art and science of foretelling the future by the lines of the hand.

The *Bible* offers a wealth of references to the human hand and its significance. We find specific references to palmistry in Job 37:7 ('He sealeth up the hand of every man; that all men may know his work.') and in Proverbs 3:16 ('Length of days *is* in her right hand; *and* in her left hand riches and honour.'). Exodus 7:5 speaks of the hand as signifying God's presence and power, Ezra 7:9 as a sign of His benevolence, and Isaiah 8:11 portrays the hand as a conveyor of God's thoughts and wishes: 'For the Lord spake thus to me with a strong hand, and instructed me that I should not walk in the way of this people . . .

The hand has also been seen as symbolizing the passion of Christ, and His hands (as those of Mary) have often been portrayed with healing light radiating from their hands and fingers. The early Catholics saw a special meaning in the fingers of the hand. The thumb signified the chief person of the Godhead, while the index finger represented the Holy Ghost. The middle finger was seen as the Christ, while the ring and little fingers revealed His double nature, divine and human respectively. Even today it is customary for a priest to bless his parishioners with the thumb, index finger and middle finger raised, symbolizing the Father, the Son, and the Holy Ghost.

Among the Muslims the hand is also considered important from a religious point of view. The hand itself is seen as a sign of protection, and often tiny plastic models of hands grace the sun visors of buses and automobiles in Arab countries. In the Muslim religion, the five fingers of the hand represent the different members of the Holy Family. The thumb symbolizes Mohammed, while the index finger represents the Lady Fatima. The middle finger stands for her husband Ali, while the ring and little fingers symbolize Hassan and Hussein respectively.

The fingers of the hand also represent the five principal commandments of the Islamic faith:

Thumb: Keep the feast of Ramadan
Index finger: Accomplish the pilgrimage to Mecca
Middle finger: Give alms to the poor
Ring finger: Perform all necessary ablutions
Little finger: Oppose all infidels

The hand has enjoyed special religious significance in nearly every world culture, including that of the Hindus, Egyptians, Buddhists and Native Americans. Prayer postures, including the raising of the hands and arms, holding the hands above the head, folding the hands, and clasping the hands, can be found in many of the sacred practices in the world's major religions. The *mudras* — or hand gestures — are essential to the performances of sacred dances in India and Bali. The symbolic hand movements of sorcerers, magicians, mystics and priests in blessings, invocations, baptisms and purification rites have been known throughout the world.

Since the time of Jesus, the hand has been considered important in

Figure 1.3: Two open hands reaching for each other is the sign of peace among the Sioux.

15

the role of healing. As a bridge from the psychic to the somatic (physical) sphere, the hand is seen as a power centre transmitting energy from one person to another. The practice of laying on of hands has been a primary element in such diverse disciplines as shamanistic medicine in Nepal, Africa, North America and Brazil, the healing ceremonies of the Roman Catholic Church, and the modern 'Therapeutic Touch' techniques such as those being taught at the New York University School of Nursing to medical doctors, nurses and other health professionals.

However, most of us take our hands completely for granted. From our first days, the hands' tactile role of perceiving and recognizing surfaces is essential to our growth and psychological development. Children touch everything to experience the people, objects and spaces around them, because hands are extremely sensitive to pressure, touch, vibration, temperature, pain and movement. In addition to being able to distinguish one substance or material from another (such as wool, polyester or cotton) the hands can tell — in an instant — whether a surface is hot, cold, wet, dry, sticky, oily or moist. Our sense of touch is essential for human relationships. A simple handshake can provide volumes of information about another person, and can tell us if he is warm, hostile, strong, friendly, supportive or weak, all within a fraction of a second.

As a working tool, the hand is a magnificent piece of equipment. As we have an opposed thumb — unlike the apes — we can hold objects, touch them on all sides at once, and use them more as an extension of the hand than merely an element for touch. The hands form a highly complex and adaptable work unit. Whether used in surgery, sports, massage or calligraphy, the human hand helps us realize the peak of our creative potential.

Finally, the hands are vital for their ability — in conjunction with the brain — to express *who we are.* By the time we are twelve to fourteen months old, psychologists say that our hands have begun to express feelings of need, joy, sorrow, anger, surprise and caring. They serve as vital components in everyday speech and enable us to express our deepest emotions to others.

The concept that our hands express who we are forms the foundation of psychologically-oriented hand analysis (chirology) as opposed to predictive palmistry or chiromancy. Although our manner of walking, facial expression and posture all express our inner being to some extent, the hands are far more expressive, more specific, and can reflect the essence of our lives with greater depth and accuracy than any other part of the body. This fact impressed the noted psychiatrist Carl Jung to such a degree that he decided to study psycho-chirology himself. In the introduction he prepared for *The Hands of Children* by Julius Speer, Jung wrote:

> . . . Hands, whose shape and functioning are so intimately connected with the psyche, might provide revealing, and therefore interpretable expressions of psychological peculiarity, that is, of human character.

Why is this? As our basic instrument of touch, the hand plays a leading role in conditioning the brain, body and emotions to develop certain responses to the world around us. In addition to being a mirror of our inherent genetic makeup, the hands can also reveal changing patterns of health, emotional stability, the development of talents, and major events which are determined by the way we respond to our life experience. Since the lines of the hand have the ability to change, they offer us a special opportunity to monitor our life path, and see into the past, the present and the future.

Though thousands of years old, hand analysis is still a young and developing science. Although we still do not know the *why* and *how* the hands reveal what they do, a complex system has evolved over the centuries that can show — through the study of the hand's shape, texture, contours and lines — important information about our lives which can serve as a signpost for self-understanding and personal fulfilment.

Unlike other books which deal primarily with the predictive aspects of hand reading, our work will focus largely on hand analysis as a tool for self-knowing. This more psychologically-oriented discipline of hand analysis can be of value in a number of ways:

1. Hand analysis helps people to develop self-recognition on a deep level. It can indicate strengths and weaknesses, point out lessons we need to learn in life, and reveal the major inner issues we need to resolve. It also teaches that conflict has a benign purpose in life and helps us develop wisdom, courage and experience.

2. It can offer a perspective on life that is both objective and real. Hand reading goes beyond our limited ego patterns and projections and gives us an idea of where we are in life and where we are going. It shows how our basic psychological nature can affect our health, career and relationships, and can indicate what is needed to achieve a greater sense of harmony and balance in our lives.

3. Because palmistry often confirms our basic insights and inner feelings, it can bring a greater degree of self-confidence and self-reliance. This enables us to look at our lives with a deeper sense of ease, and helps us work through challenges and obstacles with optimism and purpose.

4. Hand analysis enables the person to determine the types of activities to pursue in life which will bring the greatest amount of pleasure, interest and self-fulfilment.

5. Hand analysis can reveal how our experiences fit into an overall pattern of events which constitute our basic life structure or life plan. It helps us see life more in terms of an adventure to be experienced than an endless series of problems, obstacles and punishments.

6. Palmistry enables those we counsel to get in touch with their deeper essence which goes beyond the ego consciousness. It helps them to draw from this well-spring of strength and inner wisdom so that they can move courageously through periods of difficulty.

7. In addition to helping the person for whom we are reading, chirology helps the reader reach a deeper level of inner attunement with the 'client' rather than project our own subconscious assumptions into what should or should not be done in his or her life. It helps us understand their real needs and arrive at an appropriate recommendation for therapy or care.

8. For those who are serious about developing their knowledge of chirology to help others, hand analysis helps us to get more deeply

in touch with our own inner being, and leads us to rely more on our intuition and inner wisdom in our work.

This book is divided into four basic parts. The first part provides a thorough grounding in the essentials of hand analysis. The chapters that make up this first section focus on the meaning of the hand shape and consistency, the fingers, mounts and lines.

The second section concentrates on the more psychological aspects of hand reading and how they relate to our inner worlds of intelligence, will and sexuality.

The third section features the role of hand analysis in helping us achieve fulfilment in daily life, including career, health and spirituality.

The final part offers practical guidance to the prospective hand reader, including basic orientation and methodology, the taking of hand prints and organizing data, and the analysis of several interesting hands.

Chapter 2

PSYCHOLOGICAL HAND TYPES

Walter Sorell, the distinguished author of *The Story of the Human Hand* wrote 'The shape and appearance of the hand are to many of us so expressive that we instantly accept them as an indicator of personality.' He added that, although we would be mistaken to believe that we can evaluate personality by the shape of the hands alone, it is an important first step towards laying the foundation for a total personality analysis.

Over the years, many hand readers have sought to classify the hands into distinct categories. While no single system is perfect — and few hands actually conform to one specific hand type — classifying the hands gives us a general framework through which we can base a thorough hand analysis.

Basically, there are two groups of hands, which can be classified as *receptive* and *realistic*.

The *receptive* hand is often fragile and delicate in appearance, and is usually long and conic in shape. Its owners tend to be highly sensitive and emotional, with many currents affecting their lives. A rich line pattern — signifying many interests and paths of expression — is common.

The *realistic* hand is characterized by its more assertive, outgoing features. This type of hand is generally square and broad, giving an impression of being energetic, impatient, and well grounded in three-dimensional reality. Its owners tend to be robust, active and determined.

Though over a hundred years old, many hand analysts find that the system developed by Captain Stanislaus d'Arpentigny offers the most useful guidance for classifying hands. First introduced in his book *La chirognamie, ou l'art de reconnaître les tendances d'intelligence d'après les formes de la main* (Paris: Charles Le Clere, 1843), d'Arpentigny believed that there are six types of hands: elementary, spatulate, square, knotty, conic and sensitive or psychic. He later added a seventh category for 'mixed' hands.

The system we will use in this book involves four of the major hand types of d'Arpentigny, including the square, spatulate, conic and psychic. We will also focus on the mixed hand classification in which the majority of people belong. We will discuss the important modifying factors — including hand size, consistency, skin texture and flexibility — and how they can provide an accurate character analysis.

THE SQUARE HAND: 'ESTABLISH THE PLAN'

The first category in the realistic classification is the square hand type (Figure 2.1). Known by its apparent squareness in form with squared-off fingertips, it is the hand of the organizer and planner.

Owners of this hand love order, method and stability. Common sense rules their emotions and they have a steady, systematic approach to life. They don't like confusion, and often have difficulty adapting to new circumstances, especially when the hand and/or thumb is rigid. They are often thorough, competent and very careful with money.

Often lacking in spontaneity, people with square hands prefer rules, methods and structures. The German chirologist Ernst Issberner-Haldane remarked that they make excellent engineers, doctors and bureaucrats. Square hands also give their owners an inordinate ability to persevere, and to cope with difficult situations, provided that they are stable and predictable in nature.

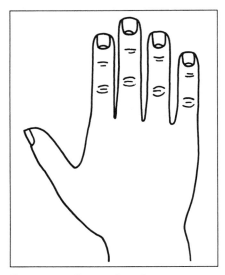

Figure 2.1: Square hand.

THE SPATULATE HAND: ACTION!

Spatulate hands (Figure 2.2) also fall into the realistic category. In appearance, they are often broad and strong, with slightly knotted fingers. Their outstanding visual quality is a marked 'fanning out' of the fingertips in the form of a spatula.

The best word to describe this hand is *action*. People with spatulate hands are energetic, tenacious, innovative, and self-confident. Like those with square hands, they are often very practical and 'grounded' in day-to-day reality.

People with spatulate hands tend to be creative and impulsive. They are generally extroverted, dynamic and exciting to be with. They often have an uncanny ability to take advantage of a situation and use it to practical advantage.

The spatulate hand is primarily a sensate hand and favours activities on the material plane. Commerce, banking, construction and entrepreneurship are popular areas of career interest for those with spatulate hands. When flexible and pliable, however, a spatulate hand increases an interest in sensual pleasures at the expense of work and other responsibilities.

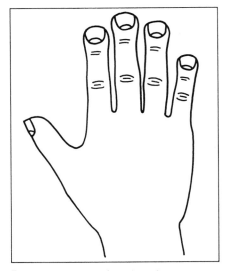

Figure 2.2: Spatulate hand.

THE CONIC HAND: LOVER OF BEAUTY

Unlike the previous hand types, conic or *artistic* hands (Figure 2.3) are of the receptive category. They tend to be slightly tapered at the base of the palm and at the tips of the fingers. The skin texture is usually fine, denoting sensitivity and a love of beauty.

People with conic hands are governed by impulse and first impressions. Unlike those with squarish hands who are ruled by reason, they are sentimental, intuitive, impulsive, capricious and romantic.

Inconsistency is said to be a major problem with those who possess conic hands. They often begin a project with great enthusiasm and then leave it for someone else to complete, especially if their hands are flexible. Although they tend to support the efforts of others, they shift loyalties often and have difficulty with commitment.

Creativity is high. If the hand is firm and the lines well formed, creative energies are channelled to mostly intellectual pursuits. When the hand is bland and fat, there is a strong sensuous nature. Rich foods, money, abundant sex, and comfortable surroundings are counted among their primary needs.

THE PSYCHIC HAND: PAINFULLY IDEALISTIC

The psychic or *intuitive* hand (Figure 2.4) is relatively rare, but quite distinctive. The hand is beautifully formed, and features long, graceful fingers with pointed tips. Like people with conic hands, their owners are very sensitive and have a strong interest in beauty. There is also a tendency to be highly strung and impressionable.

People with psychic hands are motivated by their deepest feelings. They are highly creative and possess a strong imagination. Common sense is not one of their primary attributes, and they often have trouble dealing with the 'nuts and bolts' of life.

Being 'grounded' in the material world is an important need for people with psychic hands. While they need to deepen their love of beauty and their innate interest in spiritual matters, they also need to learn how to function in the daily world. For that reason, strong and steady friends are needed to help them deal with life's practical matters.

THE MIXED HAND

Very few hands actually conform to any of the previous hand types in their pure form, although one type may predominate over the others. For this reason we have a fifth classification — the mixed hand — which can provide an important frame of reference for an accurate hand analysis.

By definition, the mixed hand (Figure 2.5) contains aspects found in two or more of the previous hand types. The hand may be primarily square, yet one or two fingers can be spatulate in shape. The basic shape of a hand may be conic, yet it may also contain elements found in the more practical square hand.

The basic shape of the hand should serve as the foundation of a careful hand analysis. The fingers, mounts and lines, as well as modifiers like hand consistency and size, skin texture, and flexibility can often provide more specific information regarding character analysis and individual life expression.

For these reasons we need to take *all* factors into account when we study a hand, and evaluate the *relationships* between the various aspects of the hand. While this may appear bewildering at first, you can accomplish this goal by cultivating intuition and patience. After some practice you can achieve a basic 'gestalt' of the hand after a few minutes of careful observation.

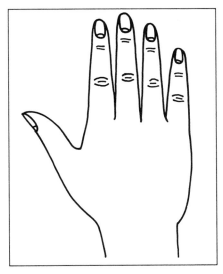

Figure 2.3: Conic hand.

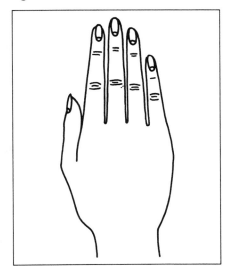

Figure 2.4: Psychic hand.

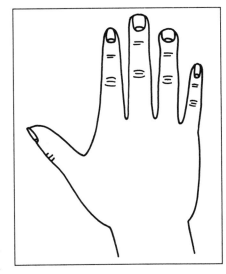

Figure 2.5: Mixed hand.

CONSISTENCY

Consistency of the hands is determined by measuring their hardness or softness under pressure. Understanding the basic consistency of the hand helps us determine both energy level and how it is expressed in daily life. By taking your friend's hands in yours and gently squeezing them, you can gain an accurate idea about their consistency.

You can identify a *flabby hand* when the flesh easily crushes together when you squeeze gently. Such a hand betrays low physical energy, and as a result the individual has difficulty manifesting both feelings and concrete plans in the material world. In many cases, flabby hands are an indication of an idle, sensitive dreamer who dislikes both physical and emotional exertion.

When the hands are flabby and thick, the sensate aspects of the personality are more pronounced. Over-indulgence in food, sex, drugs and alcohol is common, and unless the thumb is strong, willpower is often absent. When the hands are thin and weak, the energy level of the individual is extremely low. People with such hands find it extremely difficult to sustain any long-term activity.

Soft hands show a lack of bony feeling under pressure. Although soft hands can also reveal a deficient energy level, there is far more potential for movement than among their flabby-handed counterparts. When the hands are soft and thick, earlier comments regarding over-indulgence are applicable.

Elastic hands cannot be easily crushed by your grasp, and tend to spring back under pressure. They show vitality, adaptability and movement. In addition to strengthening the qualities revealed by the mounts, fingers and lines, they are found on people who like to invent and create. They have an ability to respond easily to new ideas and adapt to unexpected circumstances.

Firm hands are slightly elastic, and yield to moderate pressure. They reveal an energetic, active and strong individual, who is both responsible and stable. While not as able to adapt to new ideas and unexpected circumstances as those with elastic hands, people with firm hands are able to take account of *what is* and adapt accordingly, even though such an effort may take time.

Hard hands show no sign of yielding under pressure. Found mostly on men, these hands show no elasticity and are often coarse in texture. As can be imagined, people with hard hands also lack mental flexibility and tend to be very set in their ways. In addition, they are often prone to 'hold in' their energy, which can result in sudden outbursts of temper and stress-related diseases.

FLEXIBILITY

Hand flexibility can be determined by the ease with which it bends backward. William G. Benham, in his classic text *The Laws of Scientific Hand Reading*, wrote that the flexibility of the hand reveals 'the degree of flexibility in the mind and nature, and the readiness with which this mind has power to unfold itself and "see around the corner" of things'.

A *very flexible hand* can bend back to nearly a ninety-degree angle with a minimum of pressure. It reveals a person who is highly impressionable, easily ordered about by others, and who has difficulty being committed to one activity at a time. Such an individual frequently spends money faster than it is earned, and can be very unpredictable with both feelings and actions. If the thumb bends back easily as well, the person is generous to the extreme, and can be easily taken advantage of by others.

A *moderately flexible hand* bends back in a graceful arc (Figure 2.6). The owner of this type of hand can easily adapt to new and unforeseen circumstances. The mind is versatile, intuitive and impressionable. While it may be easy to feel, think and act, there is nevertheless the danger of becoming involved in too many activities at the same time without being committed to one or two.

A *firm hand* hardly bends back at all under pressure. Although such a hand reveals an abundance of vital force, there is a marked tendency to be careful with feelings, which are often kept hidden from view. While people with firm hands are open to new ideas, they are rarely impulsive and adapt to new circumstances and unfamiliar surroundings with difficulty.

A *stiff hand* (Figure 2.7) is extremely rigid, and may actually turn inward in its natural state. While this hand reveals a person who is extremely cautious, highly responsible and dedicated to hard work, stiff hands betray a rigid character structure. Their owners are stubborn, set in their ways, and have difficulty responding to new ideas and unexpected situations. People with stiff hands are often secretive, and have difficulty sharing their problems and feelings with others.

Although they will be discussed in greater detail later, there are several additional modifying factors which deserve brief mention at this time.

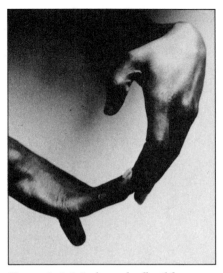

Figure 2.6: Moderately flexible hand.

Figure 2.7: Stiff hand.

HAND SIZE

The size of a person's hand is another indication of character. It can be determined in the context of the person's overall size, including height, weight and bone structure. Generally speaking, small hands reveal an individual who views life on a *grand scale*. While harbouring a basic aversion to details and minutiae (unless their fingers are knotted) people with small hands tend to perceive the *totality* of what interests them, be it a flower, a creative project, or a scientific theory.

People with *large hands* appear to gravitate more towards small things. While a woman with small hands would admire a large building in its entirety, her large-handed companion would probably focus her attention on the brass plaque by the main entrance. Large hands are often found on watchmakers, mathematicians, surgeons and others who are drawn to detailed work.

Unlike the apparently contradictory aspects of small and large hands, narrow and broad hands reveal corresponding aspects of the personality. *Narrow hands* reveal a narrow, restricted way of looking at life, which is accentuated if the hands are also stiff and hard. Conversely, *broad* hands reflect a person who is broad-minded, tolerant, and interested in new concepts and trends.

TEXTURE

Aspects of skin texture also correspond with their emotional counterpart. The softer and finer the skin, the greater the degree of physical and emotional sensitivity. Coarse skin texture reveals a more 'rough and tumble' individual, who is not strongly influenced by his or her emotional or physical surroundings.

RIGHT OR LEFT?

When we examine a person's hands, we need to discover which of the two is dominant. The non-dominant or *passive* hand reflects our past and our innate potential, while the dominant or *active* hand shows primarily what we are doing with our lives at the moment. Very often the hands reveal marked differences between our innate potential and the degree to which it is being fulfilled.

Generally speaking, the dominant hand is the hand we write with. In the rare instances when a person is ambidextrous and writes with both hands, we need to observe both hands together. When the hands are different, we should ask questions as we proceed with the reading in order to discover which of the two hands is dominant.

Chapter 3

MOUNTS AND VALLEYS

The topography of the hand can be compared to the mountains, valleys and plains of the Earth. Like the general outline of the hand discussed in the previous chapter, the regions and mounts of the hand have much to tell us about our personality traits, innate talents, and energy level.

The hand is divided into six primary zones and then into eight mounts, very much like the division of a geographic region into counties and towns. While the six zones provide a general orientation regarding latent capacities and outward expression, the eight mounts reveal the far more specialized information we need for a thorough character analysis.

THE LONGITUDINAL ZONES

The three longitudinal zones are formed by drawing an imaginary vertical line from a point between the index and middle fingers downwards towards the wrist, and another to the wrist from a point between the middle and ring fingers, as shown in Figure 3.1.

The first division forms the *active conscious* zone, which represents the energy we consciously apply in our dealings with the material world. It relates to the assertion of the ego in daily life both on an intellectual and concrete level. It is the region of practical knowledge, outward movement, and the application of principles in our work, study and relationships.

The zone located on the opposite third of the hand represents our hidden energy reserve, or the *passive subconscious*. It relates more to our innate creativity, emotional awareness and instinctual capacity.

The middle zone, or *zone of balance*, serves as a meeting place where these different energies can blend. This is an area where we often find the line of Saturn or line of life task, which moves up from the base of the palm towards the middle finger. It speaks of career, movement in life, and the degree to which we have found our life task or niche in the world.

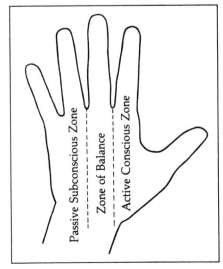

Figure 3.1: The longitudinal zones of the hand.

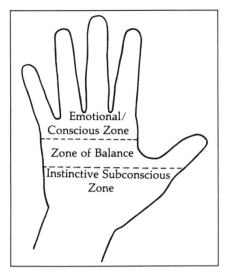

Figure 3.2: The latitudinal zones of the hand.

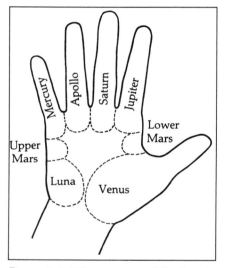

Figure 3.3: The mounts of the hand.

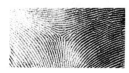

Figure 3.4: The apex of the mount.

THE LATITUDINAL ZONES

The three latitudinal zones (Figure 3.2) are formed by drawing a horizontal line from the tip of the thumb across to a point below the base of the fingers, and another from just above the thumb ball directly across the palm.

The first division, or the *emotional/conscious zone*, represents our active link with the world around us. Depending on the mounts which lie within this area, it is the zone of emotional expression, the application of power, inspiration, ambition, artistic creation and business acumen. According to Walter Sorell, it is the area of the hand that has the keenest sense of touch and holds the strongest power of connection with objects and people.

The lower region or *instinctive subconscious zone* is the zone of the Freudian 'id' and our primary motivating forces. Depending on the mounts which lie within it, this zone relates to intuition, imagination, libido, and our deepest, most hidden desires.

Like the middle vertical zone mentioned earlier, the middle horizontal zone is the practical *zone of balance*. It is the region of logic, common sense and reason, and represents the blending of thought and feeling. It is the area which filters and absorbs our subconscious drives and helps guide them towards concrete expression. It integrates our aspirations and intellectual abilities with our physical and instinctual drives.

THE MOUNTS

Each of the mounts has a name, and characterizes the type of energy that is channelled through that part of the hand. They are named after planets, which are, in turn, named after Greek and Roman gods and goddesses. They represent aspects of our character that are symbolized by these mythological beings.

The strength of a particular mount depends on its relative size when compared with the outer mounts of the hand. The more directly the mount is centred under the corresponding finger, the greater its strength and influence on the personality. You can determine the displacement of the mount by locating its *apex*. The apex of a mount is found where the ridges of the skin meet to form a pattern, as seen in Figure 3.4. If the apex of the Saturn mount, for example, is located more towards the mount of Apollo, it will take on some of the characteristics of the Apollo mount.

It should be remembered that the strength of a particular mount can be modified by other aspects of the hand, such as the shape and strength of the corresponding finger as well as the clarity and strength of both major and minor lines.

Jupiter

The mount of Jupiter is located beneath the index finger, and is named after Jupiter or Zeus, the king of the gods. The essential qualities of this mount reflect the outgoing aspects of life: generosity, gregariousness, charisma, inspiration and magnanimity. The mount of Jupiter also reveals our degree of self-confidence, leadership ability, executive skills, ambition, and religious inspiration.

When the Jupiter mount is in harmonious balance with the other mounts, it represents the positive aspects of Jupiter: healthy self assertion, a positive outlook towards life, idealism, and the desire to move out to others and help them.

If this mount is unusually strong and prominent, ambition plays a major role in the person's life. Egotism, vanity and pride are strong aspects of the personality, along with a tendency to be domineering and overbearing. If the essential qualities of this mount are complemented by the fingers and lines, strong leadership and executive skills are indicated. When modified by other aspects of the hand, positive Jupiterian traits can be distorted, and can lead to a potential for greed, selfishness, arrogance and gluttony.

If this mount is deficient or flat, the individual is likely to have a poor self-image. Unless modified by other aspects, there is a lack of ambition and the drive to succeed. Such a person often feels awkward socially and has difficulty taking advantage of new opportunities.

Saturn

The mount of Saturn is named after the god Saturn, the judge, and is found under the middle finger. While Jupiter represents the outgoing aspects of life, Saturn is more representative of the inward, self-directed side of the personality. When viewed in its positive light, the mount of Saturn symbolizes introspection, responsibility, healthy self-preservation, and the inner search for truth. As a balancing force in the human personality, it enables us to sift through life's often conflicting currents, influences and desires so that we can deal with them in a rational way.

A normal mount of Saturn reveals a lover of independence and solitude, who is able to balance the desire to be alone with the need to share the company of others. Fidelity, constancy, self-awareness, prudence and emotional balance are favoured by a medium-sized mount of Saturn, along with an ability to study and explore new ideas.

A highly developed mount often accentuates and distorts Saturn's essential qualities, especially if modified by other factors. Prudence can yield to fearful withdrawal, and healthy introspection can be overtaken by a tendency to be over-analytical and too self-absorbed. A strong Saturn mount can be found on many people who are rigid, taciturn and defensive.

Apollo

Apollo is the god of power and self-expression, and his mount is located under the ring finger. While Western hand readers relate this mount to all forms of creativity — especially in the fields of art and music — Hindu chirologists call this mount the *Vidja Sthana*, ruling education and scholarship.

A medium-sized mount of Apollo reveals a deep love of beauty and strong creative ability. This creative ability need not be restricted to art or music, but can include cooking, acting, writing and design. If a person has an attractive home or dresses well, chances are that he or she has a well-developed mount of Apollo.

Like the mounts of Jupiter and Saturn, a very large mount of Apollo can both strengthen and distort its basic 'core' qualities. A preoccupation with pleasure, wealth or fame are often revealed by a very prominent Apollo mount. A strong love of beauty can become a devotion to appearance values and living on the periphery. Vanity and self-indulgence can replace the natural desire to look after our appearance and take good care of ourselves.

When this mount is weak, the individual is lacking in the essential Apollonian qualities. Instead of being exciting and filled with beauty, the person's life is ascetic, boring, and 'flat'. Deficiency in this mount can also indicate low physical energy.

Mercury

Mercury was the messenger of the gods. For this reason the mount of Mercury, located under the little finger, rules communication and the objectification of life principles into spoken and written words. It is the mount of commerce, writing, medicine, mathematics and diplomacy. Mercury also governs sagacity and the ability to judge human nature. Perhaps this is why the Hindus call this mount *Jaya Sthana* or 'the place of victory'.

A well-developed mount of Mercury — especially when accompanied by a long finger — points towards commercial talent and oratorical skill. Actors, diplomats, salespeople, and public speakers, almost always possess a strong mount of Mercury.

A very prominent mount has no negative aspects by itself, although its positive qualities can be modified by a poorly-formed Mercury finger. The fingers and their meaning will be examined in detail in the following chapter.

A small, flat mount of Mercury — especially if accompanied by a short or weak finger — reveals a lack of commercial and scientific ability. Communication with others on a one-to-one basis may also be a problem, especially in the context of an affective relationship.

Mars

There are two mounts of Mars on the hand. Both reflect the qualities of Mars, the god of war. The mounts of Mars represent essentially the dynamic, egotistical and separative aspects of the personality. These mounts speak of our desire to survive, to move forward, and to overcome obstacles and difficulties.

The *upper mount of Mars* is located just under the mount of Mercury, and symbolizes determination and resistance. When well-formed and hard to the touch, it reflects a person who is both courageous and stubborn, who resists being used or manipulated by others. A small or soft mount reveals a lack of valour and resistance. When found on a soft and flexible hand, the person is easily 'pushed around' and has difficulty standing up for his or her rights. When this mount is extremely large and hard, violence and brutality are major components of the individual's character.

Unlike the upper mount of Mars which symbolizes passive resistance, the *lower mount of Mars* reveals the more active and outgoing Martian

28

qualities. Found between the mounts of Jupiter and Venus, it often appears as a small tumour located just inside the thumb joint. A well-developed mount indicates strong self-assertion and the courage to face life's challenges and overcome them. When this mount is large and hard, the person has a strong temper in addition to an abundance of sexual passion (especially when accompanied by a large mount of Venus). A small or deficient mount indicates a basically quiet, passive, and introverted individual who rarely gets angry with others.

Venus

Named after the goddess of love, the mount of Venus is both an indicator of our aesthetic nature as well as our ability to love. The noted Spanish chirologist, Orencia Colomar, believes that the mount of Venus is so important that it can modify the information revealed by all the other mounts of the hand.

Ideally, the mount of Venus comprises the thumb ball and is outlined by a widely sweeping life line. The normal mount should take up approximately one-third of the palm and should neither be too hard, too bland, nor too heavily lined. A good Venus mount should be smooth and firm to the touch, higher than the other mounts in elevation, and slightly pink in colour.

A normal mount of Venus reveals warmth, vitality and energy. It shows *joie de vivre* and the ability to love and be loved. A well-formed Venus mount also strengthens the life line and reveals a strong capacity to resist disease.

When the mount is excessively large in relation to the other mounts, there is an abundance of physical passion, with a large appetite for sex, food and drink. When the mount is also hard, this passion can easily spill over into aggression and brutality, especially if the mount is reddish in colour.

A small, flat or weak Venus mount reveals a lack of vital energy and physical passion. The personality tends to be somewhat lymphatic and cold, especially if the life line cuts through the Venus mount. Very often a strong love affair can actually increase the size of this mount.

Luna

Located opposite the mount of Venus just above the wrist, the mount of Luna represents the source of the passive, receptive and emotional aspects of the personality. It is the home of our subconscious impressions and unconscious drives, instincts and imagination.

Ideally, this mount should be broad and lightly rounded in shape. It points to an interest in religion and mysticism, and a desire to perceive more than meets the eye. People with medium-sized lunar mounts have a good imagination balanced by reality.

The stronger and more prominent the mount, the greater the imagination and subconscious drives, especially if the head line slopes downward towards its centre. Intuition is enhanced, along with the potential for creation. A large mount of Luna also can reveal a strong desire to protect and nurture others, especially if accompanied by 'Samaritan lines' under the Mercury mount.

Many of the most interesting people in literature, the arts and science have well-developed mounts of Luna. When deficient or lacking, the individual tends to be too realistic, unimaginative and dull. Fantasy is of no interest to him and imagination is seen as an indulgence of fools.

DERMATOGLYPHICS

In addition to the mounts themselves, many hands reveal specific skin ridge patterns or *dermatoglyphics* which lie either on or between certain mounts.

When examining skin ridge patterns, it is important to note both their prominence and clarity. The larger and clearer they are, the more significant their meaning. If a hand does not feature specific dermatoglyphic patterns, there should be no cause for concern. Their presence serves primarily to highlight certain personality traits and offer an additional source of information for the hand analyst.

The most common skin ridge pattern on the palm is the *loop of seriousness* (Figure 3.5). Located between the fingers of Saturn and Apollo, it is found on approximately thirty-five per cent of all hands. As its name implies, this loop is a sign of a person with a predominently serious nature. People with these loops tend to be responsible, reliable, and feel the need to do something worth while with their lives. Because the loop of seriousness is often found in the hands of career or business people, it is frequently associated with money and material success.

The *loop of humour* (Figure 3.6) is located between the Apollo and Mercury fingers, and is found on perhaps fifteen per cent of hands. As opposed to the loop of seriousness, it reflects a person who has a light-hearted, happy-go-lucky approach to life. Although owners of this loop enjoy work, they often prefer pleasure and satisfaction from their career over status or financial reward. Many people with this loop possess a wonderful sense of humour, and have a strong sense of the ridiculous.

The *raja loop* (Figure 3.7) is relatively rare, and appears on fewer than one hand in a hundred. Found primarily on 'special' people who possess an unusual ability or talent, they are sometimes found on very charismatic individuals who enjoy a large public following, like a popular entertainer, military hero, or spiritual leader.

Other major patterns worth noting can be found on the mount of Luna. Any prominent marking on this mount highlights a strong imagination and/or powerful instincts:

A strong *composite* marking, known also as an 's-curve' (Figure 3.8), is linked to an adventurous personality and the love of travel. The pattern shown here belongs to Buzz Aldrin, the American astronaut. According to the noted Australian palmist Andrew Fitzherbert, a composite pattern on a man's hand will increase so-called 'feminine' attributes like gentleness and receptivity, while on a woman's hand it will highlight 'masculine' qualities like competitiveness and aggression.

An outward-moving look (or *psychic loop*) on the mount of Luna would reveal strong intuition or even psychic ability; an inward-moving loop (or *memory loop*) indicates a talent for insight into the minds and motives of others.

Both *Your Life in Your Hands* by Beryl Hutchinson and *Hand Psychology* by Andrew Fitzherbert detail further dermatoglyphic markings.

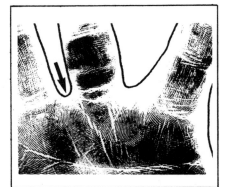
Figure 3.5: The loop of seriousness.

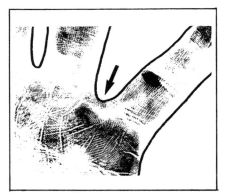
Figure 3.6: The loop of humour.

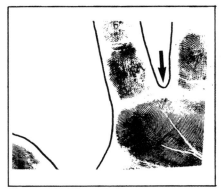
Figure 3.7: The raja loop.

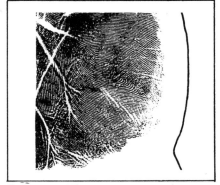
Figure 3.8: The composite marking or 'curve'.

Chapter 4
THE FINGERS

While the mounts and basic form of the hand provide the groundwork needed to help determine character, the shape, size and relative position of the fingers offer a wealth of more specific information concerning both the personality and major avenues of expression. In fact, many chirologists feel that the fingers can tell us more about a person than any other single aspect of the hand.

When studying the fingers, it is important to consider each finger by itself and also as an integral part of the hand. In addition, we must also understand the relationship of each finger to the others. We can determine the finger's relative strength in the hand by opening the palm completely, with fingers held together. If the fingers tend to lean towards one in particular, that finger is the dominant finger of the hand and provides us with the keynote of the individual's character. Figure 4.1, for example, shows a hand with a dominant Saturn influence, because the other fingers (including a strong Jupiter finger) bend towards Saturn.

Before we discuss the characteristics of each individual finger, it is important to become familiar with the appearance of the fingers in general.

Flexibility: Like the hands, the degree of flexibility of the fingers provides important clues to the person's character and its ability to adapt. Ideally, the fingers should arch gently backward, revealing a capacity to adapt easily to new ideas and situations. When the top phalange of the finger bends back as well, strong creative talent is present. When the tip of the Mercury finger bends back, for example, it is a sign of writing ability.

Length and Width: The length of the fingers must be judged in relation to the length of the palm. A balance would exist if the size of the middle or Saturn finger were the same length as the palm itself.

Generally speaking, people with short fingers (Figure 4.2) are intuitive, impatient, impulsive, and are able to quickly grasp the essential points of an issue. They see things on a large scale, be they philosophical concepts, projects to be undertaken, or panoramic views of the countryside. Unless their fingers are knotted, they also tend to overlook details.

Long fingers (Figure 4.3) indicate opposite qualities. Patience, love

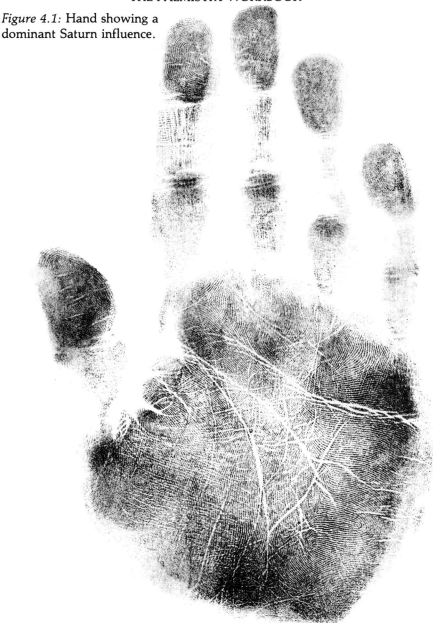

Figure 4.1: Hand showing a dominant Saturn influence.

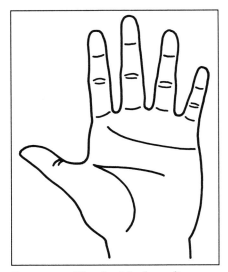

Figure 4.2: Hand with short fingers.

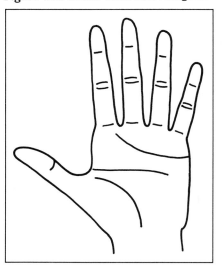

Figure 4.3: Hand with long fingers.

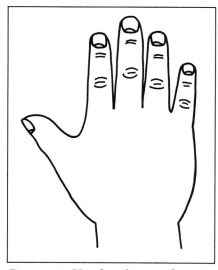

Figure 4.4: Hand with smooth fingers.

of detail and analysis are common traits of long-fingered people. They like to focus on the minutiae of daily life, and tend to relate to the world in more of an intellectual than intuitive context. Long fingers often promote an introspective nature, with the tendency to hold grudges and harbour resentment.

People with thick, fleshy fingers have a basically sensate nature. They enjoy luxury, good food, and pleasure. Thin fingers tend to reveal a more intellectual person, who is often removed from the three-dimensional world.

Knuckles: Smooth fingers (Figure 4.4) have an absence of developed joints, and indicate a tendency to be intuitive and impulsive. People with smooth fingers often have difficulty breaking down a problem into its component parts and are impatient with details. Their decisions are based primarily on hunches rather than a careful analysis of the facts.

Psychologically, they are often in touch with their feelings and find it easy to express their anger, love or joy.

If the fingers are both short and smooth, impulsiveness, impatience and aversion to detail are accentuated, while long fingers will tend to strengthen the intellectual and analytical aspects of the personality.

Knotty fingers which are not due to arthritis (Figure 4.5) reveal a person with a strong analytical mind. Their owners are rarely seduced by appearances and tend to penetrate deeply into an issue, using logic, detail, and analysis. On a psychological level, people with knotty fingers tend to lack spontaneity and find it difficult to express their feelings to others.

The Phalanges: The index, middle, ring and little fingers are divided into three parts or *phalanges* (Figure 4.6). The top phalange is that of mental order, the middle phalange is that of practical order, while the bottom phalange is called the phalange of material order.

When the top phalange is the longest of the three, it is an indication that mental activities absorb most of the person's attention. A long middle phalange indicates that the primary keynote — as expressed by the particular finger's significance — is action. A long and thick phalange of material order reflects that the person is more grounded in the material or instinctual aspects of life. Remember that the comparative length of the phalanges may vary from finger to finger.

Before we proceed to the individual fingers, let us recapitulate the key qualities of the various types:

Spatulate (Figure 4.7): Energetic, active, realistic, impulsive, down-to-earth, self-confident.
Square (Figure 4.8): Loves order and regularity, perseverance, foresight, structured, rational decisive action.
Conic (Figure 4.9): Artistic, receptive to outer stimuli, sensitive, restless, impulsive, instinctual.
Psychic (Figure 4.10): Strongly affected by outside stimuli, sensitive, dreamy, intuitive, mediumistic.
Round (Figure 4.11): Adaptable, well-rounded, balanced, active yet receptive, mental yet emotional.

Many hands are a combination of these types, so we need to take into account both the qualities governing each individual finger as well as the finger's basic form. Now let us consider each finger individually.

THE THUMB

In Hindu palmistry, the thumb is considered so important that many hand readers restrict themselves to studying the thumb alone when they analyze character.

The thumb relates to our ego strength and our level of energy or life force. Because it permits us to accomplish a wide variety of tasks in daily life, the thumb also symbolizes our ability to express this energy and power in the world.

The size of the thumb is an index to the basic energy level of the

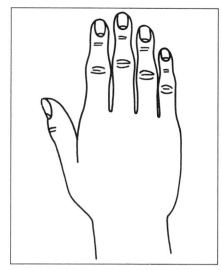

Figure 4.5: Knotted hand.

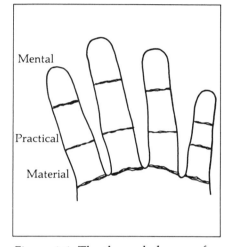

Figure 4.6: The three phalanges of the fingers. Mental, Practical, Material.

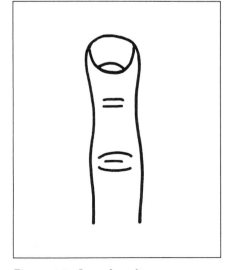

Figure 4.7: Spatulate finger.

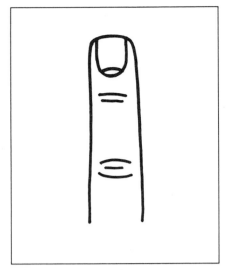

Figure 4.8: Square finger.

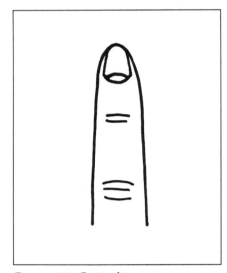

Figure 4.9: Conic finger.

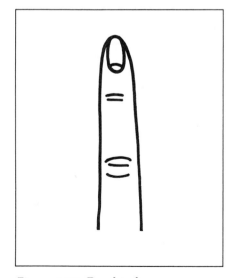

Figure 4.10: Psychic finger.

individual. Normally, the tip of the thumb reaches the lower phalange of the index (or Jupiter) finger. A long thumb (Figure 4.12) (often known as a 'capable' thumb) indicates an abundance of energy in addition to a forceful personality. People like Voltaire, Newton and Leibnitz were said to possess large thumbs, as their strong personalities confirmed.

Individuals with short thumbs (Figure 4.13) tend to be weak-willed and are not known for strong character. They often lack self-confidence, forcefulness, and an ability to follow through with a project or endeavour.

However, before we proclaim a thumb to be long or short, we need to take account of how the thumb is set on the hand. A *low-set thumb* can be positioned at a ninety-degree angle to the index finger, as shown in Figure 4.14. It reveals a person who is adaptable, independent and who takes risks. To the degree that the thumb is set high in the hand (Figure 4.15) the person tends to withhold energy. There is a fear of letting go and moving with the flow of life. In popular jargon, he or she would best be described as 'uptight' unless modifying aspects of the hand are present, such as a separation between the life and head lines at their commencement.

The thumb is divided into three parts (Figure 4.16). The nail phalange is called the *phalange of will*, while the second is the *phalange of logic*. The third part is the mount of Venus, previously discussed.

A strong phalange of will — one which is well rounded, long and wide — indicates decisiveness, 'staying power', and the ability to transform thoughts into deeds. When this phalange is conic in shape, there may be a lack of resistance and the person's energy tends to scatter when confronted with a major project or serious problem requiring long-term attention. If this phalange is thin or flat (when viewed from the side), the person has a tendency to be highly strung and nervous (Figure 4.17). When the fingertip is squarish, there is an ability to organize and execute projects. A spatulate tip is the sign of a dynamic individual with a zest for living. Things 'happen' around him.

Some people have a thumb with a deformed will phalange which has a bulbous or clubbed appearance. Palmists have called it a 'Murderer's thumb (Figure 4.18) and, while it does not necessarily indicate homicidal tendencies, it is often the sign of a person who tends to withhold energy to such an extent that strong, sudden bursts of temper can result. This 'holding' of energy may also result in both physical and psychological problems.

The phalange of logic reveals our degree of reasoning power. Ideally, it should be the same length and strength as the will phalange, which would indicate a balance between thought and action. To the extent that this phalange is long and thick, the ego will exert strong control over action to the point where constant reasoning can kill movement altogether. This is especially true if the thumb joint is knotted. When the logic phalange is 'waisted' (Figure 4.19), logic is not a major aspect of the personality.

Determining the *flexibility* of the thumb is especially important to the hand reader. A supple thumb (Figure 4.20) bends back at the joint, and indicates emotional versatility and an ease to adapt. Generosity is an important component of the person's character, although such generosity is rarely indiscriminate. When extremely flexible (i.e., bending back ninety degrees or more) the person is generous to a fault, and can also be extravagant with money, especially if the rest of the hand is flexible as well. Will power is poor.

A moderately flexible thumb bends back only slightly under pressure. It reveals a practical individual who relies on common sense. While it indicates a strong and determined will, there is nevertheless a degree of open-mindedness and the ability to adapt.

A stiff thumb (Figure 4.21) will not bend back under pressure. Their owners tend to be stubborn, prudent, and have tremendous difficulty adapting to new ideas and situations. On the more positive side, people with stiff thumbs are generally very stable and highly responsible. They can be relied upon for almost anything. The qualities of a stiff thumb can be modified by a flexible hand.

JUPITER

Like its corresponding mount, the index or Jupiter finger represents leadership, ambition and the drive to succeed in life. Ideally, it should be the same length as the ring, or Apollo finger, and slightly shorter than the middle, or Saturn finger.

If Jupiter is longer than Apollo, the ego is strong, with a healthy amount of self-esteem. People with long Jupiter fingers are natural leaders, and often are involved in running a business, a school, or other job calling for executive or administrative ability. However, a long Jupiter finger (especially if it curves inward) can reveal a tendency to be vain, domineering, and controlling. To the degree that Jupiter is shorter than Apollo, there is a corresponding lack of self-esteem and self-confidence. The person tends to underestimate his or her talents and accomplishments, especially if the head and life lines join together.

To the extent that Jupiter bends towards Saturn, its essential qualities are distorted and the tendency to be possessive, jealous and acquisitive are often indicated. When the fingertip is pointed, religious and inspirational feelings are strong. When the Jupiter finger is both long and pointed, the individual can excel in the role of a religious or spiritual leader.

SATURN

The middle finger is named for Saturn, and is the finger of propriety, responsibility and introspection. It serves as the link between the subconscious aspects of the personality represented by Apollo and Mercury, and the more active, conscious qualities of the thumb and Jupiter finger.

When this finger is straight, there is a harmonious relationship between will and emotion, as well as a balance between liking to be with people and wanting to be alone. When Saturn curves slightly towards Jupiter, the personality is generally spontaneous and outgoing, and the individual enjoys being in the company of others as much as possible. A slight curve towards Apollo indicates a need to be alone more than not. A sharp curve towards Apollo is a sure indication of chronic

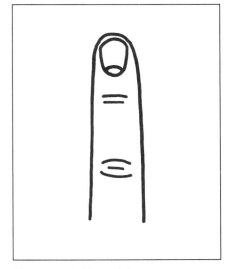

Figure 4.11: Round finger.

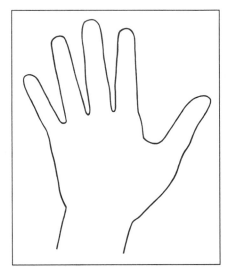

Figure 4.12: Long thumb.

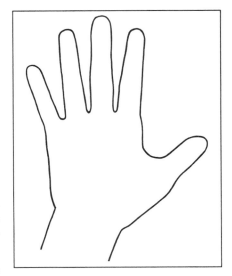

Figure 4.13: Short thumb.

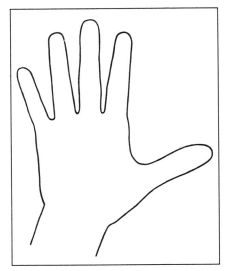

Figure 4.14: Low-set thumb.

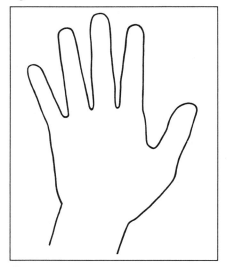

Figure 4.15: Thumb set high.

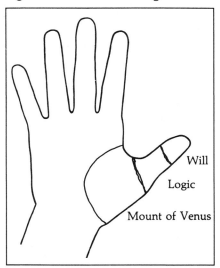

Figure 4.16: The three phalanges of the thumb.

depression. When such a formation is observed, take special care to look for confirming or modifying aspects in the rest of the hand, particularly on the head line.

APOLLO

Like its corresponding mount, the ring or Apollo finger rules creativity, the love of art and music, and the ability to express ourselves to others. A long, straight Apollo finger is found on many artists, actors and others who work primarily with the public. Many of these people also possess an Apollo finger with a spatulate tip, which favours strong communication skills.

When Apollo bends towards Saturn, there is a tendency to overestimate others, which often results in disillusion when they don't live up to our high standards. According to some chirologists, an Apollo finger which bends sharply towards Saturn is a sure indication of a gambler and libertine.

MERCURY

The ring or Mercury finger rules communication and business ability, and many successful writers, bankers and entrepreneurs have long and well-formed Mercury fingers. Ideally, this finger should reach to the top phalange of Apollo. The longer the finger, the greater the ability to communicate with others, whether in the context of writing a book or being involved in a marriage. When this finger is short, it is not easy making oneself understood, and close relationships are often difficult to establish and maintain.

A straight Mercury finger indicates honesty, frankness and trustworthiness. A slight curving towards Apollo reveals a degree of astuteness and diplomacy, while a sharp bending towards Apollo (not the result of arthritis) indicates a tendency to be manipulative and even dishonest. When the hand features a sharply-bending Jupiter finger as well, the individual would stop at nothing to obtain what he or she wants.

FINGER SPACING

When the fingers are held closely together on an open hand, the individual person would tend to be somewhat contracted and fearful, and would lack self-confidence and independence. The wider the spacing between the fingers, the greater the openness, daring and independence. When the Jupiter finger breaks away from the rest of the hand, the leadership and self-reliance are increased. To the degree that the space between the Mercury and Apollo fingers is wide, the person is an independent thinker. If the life and head lines are separate as well, independent thinking is accompanied by action.

A NOTE ABOUT NAILS

Although the fingernails are of primary value in medical diagnosis, they can also help us evaluate character.

Ideally, the nails should be slightly longer than wide, and be slightly curved as opposed to flat, as shown in Figure 4.22. People with long nails are often drawn to artistic endeavours and like to think and analyze. Narrow nails reveal an individual with a narrow, dogmatic outlook on life who is generally not very open to new ideas and trends. Broad nails reveal broadmindedness. Short nails (when not a result of nail biting) indicate an impatient and often critical personality. A more detailed analysis of the nails, accompanied by illustrations, can be found in chapter 9.

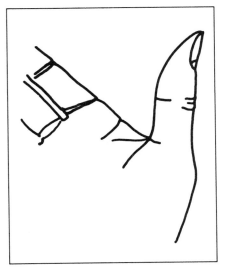

Figure 4.17: Flat thumbtip.

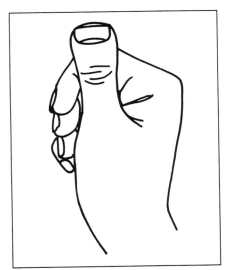

Figure 4.18: 'Murderer's' thumb.

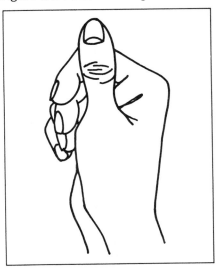

Figure 4.19: Waisted thumb.

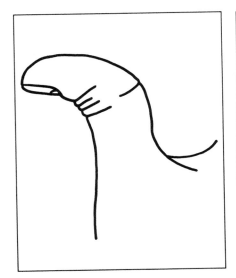

Figure 4.20: Supple thumb.

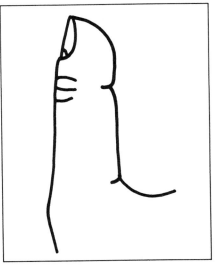

Figure 4.21: Stiff thumb.

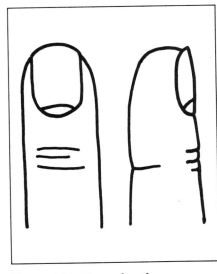

Figure 4.22: Normal nail.

FINGERPRINTS

Fingerprints are important because they represent the basic and most unchangeable aspects of the personality. Although we can learn to modify the traits the fingerprints represent, we cannot completely erase them.

There are primarily three basic types of fingerprint patterns:

The Loop

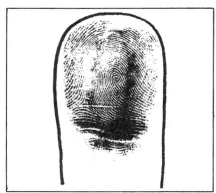

Figure 4.23: The loop.

The loop (Figure 4.23) is by far the most common fingerprint pattern. It represents an easy-going, adaptable and 'middle-of-the-road' personality. Owners of hands where loops predominate are generally easy to get along with. Positive qualities of the loop include flexibility and the ability to have a well-rounded view of things. The primary negative aspect of this pattern is the tendency to lack individuality. Wherever a loop is found, it reflects the basic 'middle ground' tendencies the particular finger represents.

High loops (Figure 4.24) are relatively rare, and are believed to be signs of high intelligence and an enthusiastic outlook on life.

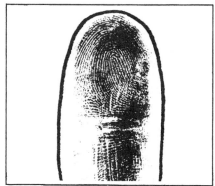

Figure 4.24: The high loop.

The Whorl

The whorl (Figure 4.25) is a sign of the individualist and the specialist. A person whose fingerprints consist mostly of whorls will tend to be his or her own person and will not conform to the standards of others. People with whorls often seek to carve out their own niche in life and become experts in some specialized area. Positive qualities of the whorl include independence, a love of freedom, and overall ability. Negative aspects include a tendency towards isolation, secretiveness, and self-obsession.

A whorl on the thumb reveals an individualistic way of doing things and strong willpower; on Jupiter, a tendency to be independent and the ability think for oneself; on Saturn, individuality in personal beliefs; on Apollo, a definite artistic ability; on Mercury, a strong talent for verbal or written expression; and on both Mercury and Apollo, a highly active subconscious mind open to precognitive dreaming and intuitive impressions.

Figure 4.25: The whorl.

The Arch

The arch (Figure 4.26) is a sign of capability and trustworthiness. People whose fingerprints are primarily of the arch pattern would tend to be hard-working, efficient and good with their hands, with possible professions as craftspeople, mechanics and surgeons. Positive aspects of the arch include steadiness, realism and usefulness, while negative traits include emotional repression, a reluctance to accept change, and difficulty in responding to new ideas or unexpected situations. Generally speaking, the higher the arch, the more skilful and idealistic the individual.

An arch on the thumb is a sure sign of a practical doer, who has a commonsense approach when dealing with new projects or when facing challenges; on Jupiter, a practical approach towards work, an ability with crafts, and a realistic view of one's ambitions and life goals; on Saturn, a practical attitude towards investments and home improvements; and on Apollo, artistic expression will probably be in an area that is sensate or useful, such as knitting or woodworking. An isolated arch on Mercury is too rare to make a general interpretation.

Figure 4.26: The arch.

Chapter 5

THE LINES

The lines of the hand can be compared to the motorways, highways and country lanes of a road map. They indicate the major talents and energies we have at our disposal, our capacity to manifest these talents in our life, and the probable directions these talents and energies will take us. In essence, the lines of the hand form a natural map of our life course, while allowing for occasional detours and changes of direction according to our free will.

Even though hand analysis dates back some seven thousand years, chirologists are not exactly certain as to *why* the lines exist. However, over the centuries a reliable system has evolved which helps us understand our physical constitution, mental and emotional characteristics, sexuality, creative ability, and the major influences which affect our lives, as well as probable travel, relationships, healing ability, psychic power, and the degree to which we are fulfilling our major goals in life. The lines not only reveal the past and the present, but provide important insights into probable future events and trends.

Nor do we fully understand how the lines are formed. Some feel that lines represent 'rivers of energy' which come through the fingers and into the palm. In any case, the form and number of lines are not dependent on hand movements, nor are they related to what we do for a living. However, sedentary individuals often have more lines than those who perform heavy manual labour.

The lines of the hand can change in a matter of weeks, although most changes can be seen every few years. They are affected by both attitude modification and changes in behaviour. Learning how to meditate, cutting down on cigarettes, or devoting more time and energy to making a relationship work can alter the lines of the hand dramatically. A case in point involves the prints of a twenty-year-old university student taken six weeks apart (Figure 5.1). During this time, the young man changed his major from business administration to inhalation therapy, became a vegetarian, began to study Theosophy and related subjects, and told his father (an Army colonel) that he was not going to join the Army Reserve as planned.

For those who are interested in achieving their full potential, the objective knowledge offered by the ever-changing lines can be both

Figure 5.1: The hands of T.K., taken six weeks apart. Note the increase in the number of lines, and the lengthening of the lines of heart, career, union and intuition. *See opposite.*

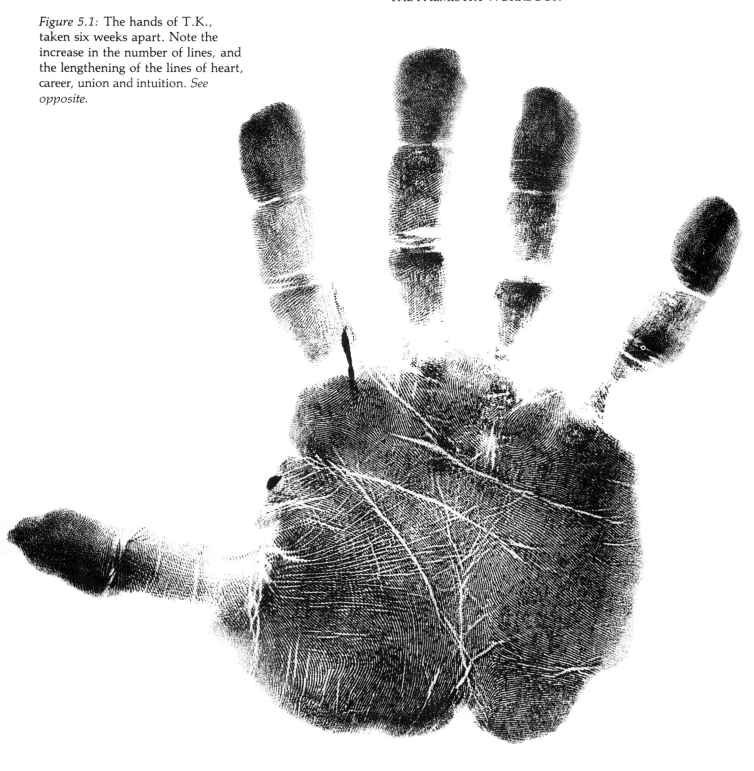

invaluable and exciting. The lines show that we are indeed the 'master of our fate' and can assume personal responsibility for our life and its direction.

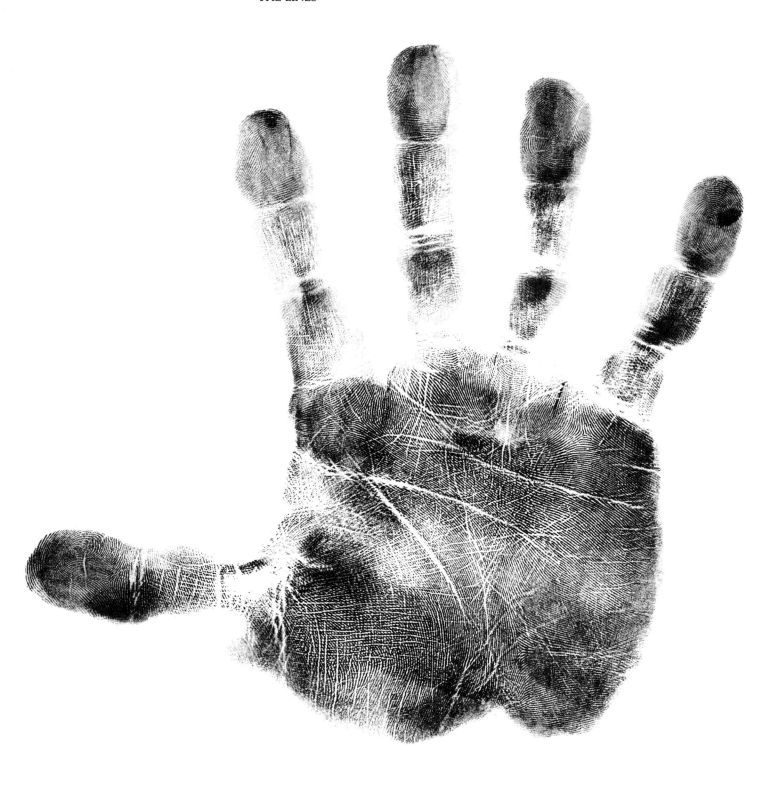

LINE QUALITY AND QUANTITY

Ideally, lines should be clear and well-defined, and have a colour

Figure 5.2: The major lines of the hand.

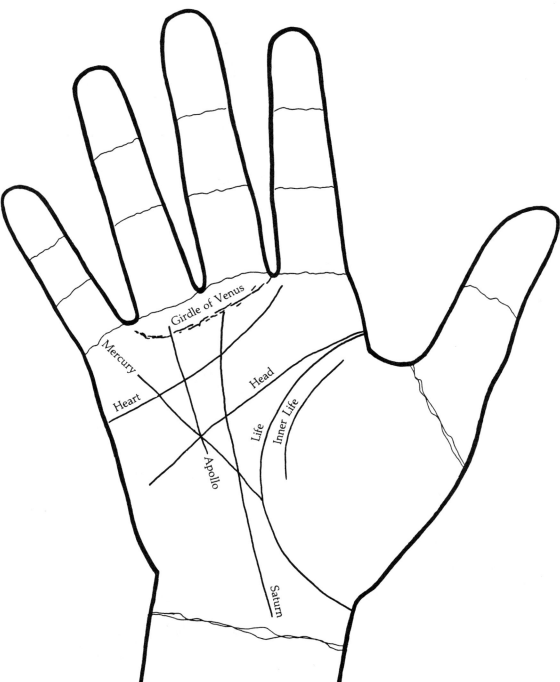

complementing that of the skin. The line's depth and width should be even. A particularly deep line reveals excessive energy, while a broad, shallow line indicates a lack of strength and focus. Generally speaking, the stronger the line, the stronger its influence.

The number of lines on the hand is also important. An abundance of lines, as shown in Figure 5.3, indicates hypersensitivity and nervousness. It can also show that the individual has many paths in life through which to express his or her talents. Few lines on the hand, as

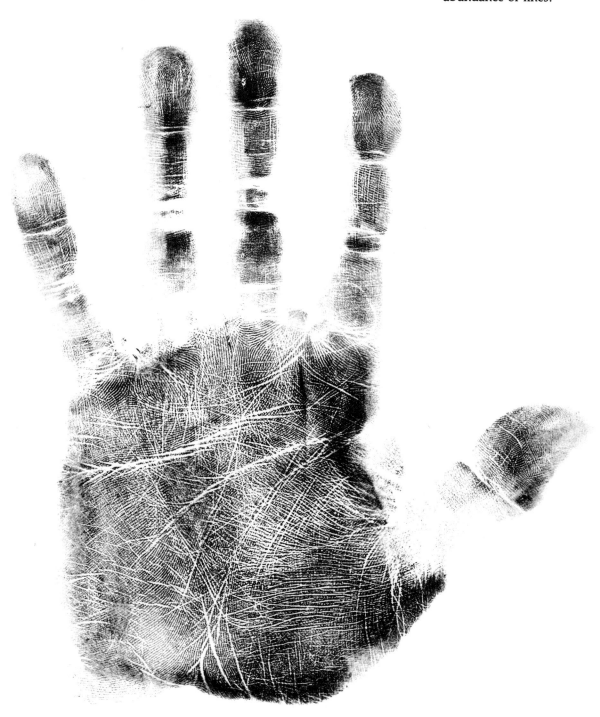

seen in Figure 5.4, generally indicates little sensitivity with few basic channels for life expression.

Before we go into detail about each of the lines, there are several important formations we need to be familiar with.

Figure 5.4: Hand showing few lines.

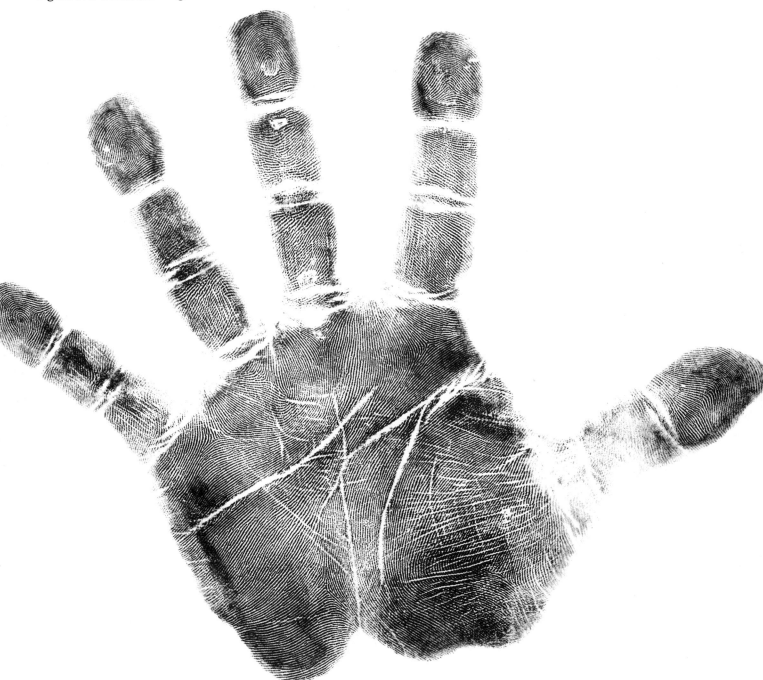

Splintering or *splitting* of a line (Figure 5.5) dissipates its strength and focus. In some cases, a split indicates a change or a new phase in a person's life, so its existence is not necessarily a negative sign.

Lines of influence (Figure 5.6) are small lines which cross or run parallel to the major lines. They will be discussed in detail towards the conclusion of this chapter.

Islands (Figure 5.7) form where there is a splitting from a line which reunites with that line later on. Islands impair the line's strength and indicate a lack of focus and dissipation of energy.

A *chain* (Figure 5.8) is composed of many islands together, and indicates a prolonged period of vacillation and scattered energy. The line as a whole is weakened as a result.

A *fork* (Figure 5.9) appears at the end of a line when the line splits. Depending on its location, it can either indicate a dissipation of the basic energies represented in the line, or can reveal balance and adaptability.

A *dot* (Figure 5.10) appears as a slight coloured indentation on the line. The existence of a dot indicates a physical or emotional setback of some kind, depending on its colour and location.

A *grille* (Figure 5.11) is formed by numerous fine lines which crisscross each other. It generally indicates a period of diffused and scattered energy.

A *square* (Figure 5.12) is formed by four independent lines which create a rectangle. It is a sign of protection and preservation and often repairs a broken line.

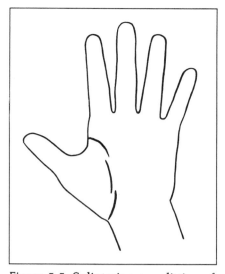

Figure 5.5: Splintering or splitting of a line.

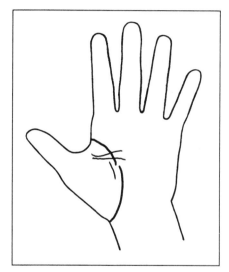

Figure 5.6: Lines of influence.

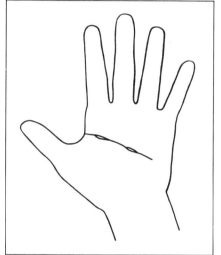

Figure 5.7: Islands.

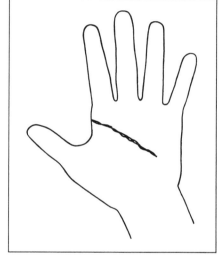

Figure 5.8: A chained line.

THE LINE OF LIFE

The life line is the principal line of the hand. It begins at the edge of the palm between the thumb and forefinger, and arcs downwards around the mount of Venus. It is our primary indicator of the strength of our physical constitution and our level of vital force. This line records periods of disease, accidents and other major events which touch our life. It also indicates the probable length of time we can expect to live. Figure 5.13 shows how to gauge time on the life and other major lines of the hand.

When attempting to determine the length of life, several factors need to be taken into account. When the life line is the same length on both hands, the ending of the line would indicate the probable time of death. However, if the lines are of different length, the line on the active hand is more likely to be correct. In addition, a long head, heart and/or career line can modify a short life line, just as an abrupt early termination of one or more of these lines can indicate a shorter life span.

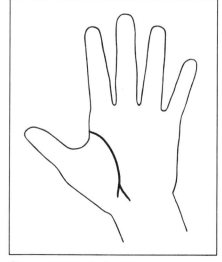

Figure 5.9: A forked line.

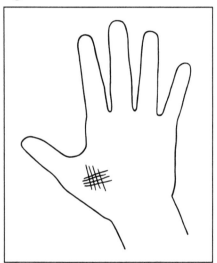

Figure 5.10: A 'dotted' line.

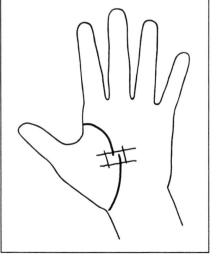

Figure 5.11: Lines forming a 'grille'.

Figure 5.12: Lines forming a 'square'.

Never predict a time of death. In the first place, there is a good chance you may be wrong. Many people with short life lines have been known to live to become great-grand-parents, while others with long life lines have been known to die far before their time. In addition, by predicting the time of death you may be planting a 'seed thought' in the person's mind which can have unfortunate self-fulfilling results. Whenever you see a short or broken life line, be sure to mention that the lines of the hand are not set in concrete and that they can change according to our attitudes and habits.

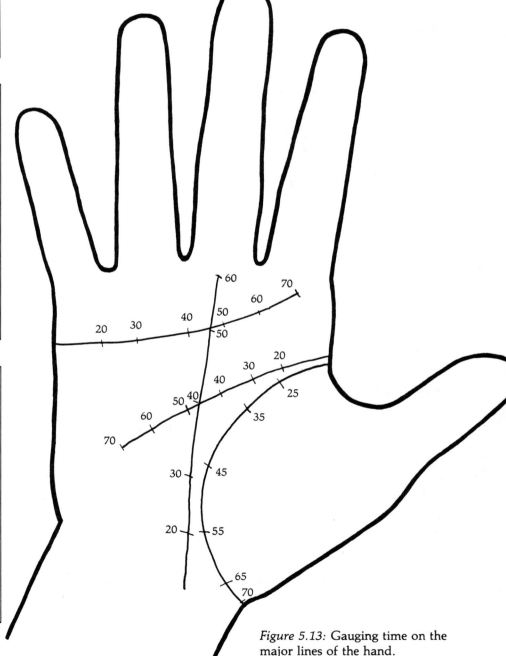

Figure 5.13: Gauging time on the major lines of the hand.

46

No two life lines are the same, although most conform to some of the following brief descriptions:

Long, clear and well-marked (Figure 5.14): Strong physical constitution, good health, vitality, resistance to disease, ability to meet life's challenges, probable long life.

Short, clear and well-marked (Figure 5.15): Intensity, good health, possible short life. See other lines for possible modifying factors.

Red and deep: Powerful energy, intensity, violent disposition. Observe other hand characteristics for possible modifying influences.

Wide, not well-marked: Personality is easily influenced by outside stimuli.

Long and weak (Figure 5.16): Weak constitution, vulnerability to disease, tendency towards nervousness and indecision.

Islands (Figure 5.17): Lapses in health or general physical weakness. Obstacles, periods of indecision or lack of focus in life.

Breaks (Figure 5.18): Interruptions in the tenor of life, either physical or psychological or both.

Separated from head line (Figure 5.19): Impulsive, impatient, self-reliant, extroverted. Can be reckless.

Connected to head line (Figure 5.20): Careful, cautious, takes a long time to make decisions. The point where the lines separate indicates the age of independence from the family physically and/or psychologically. In general, the longer the lines are connected, the longer it takes to make decisions and act independently.

Forming broad arc around Venus mount (Figure 5.21): Warm, sensual, emotionally responsive.

Hugging close to thumb, cutting into Venus mount (Figure 5.22): Inhibited, cold, unresponsive.

Moving towards mount of Luna (Figure 5.23): Naturally restless disposition.

Branch from life line moving up towards Jupiter (Figure 5.24): Optimism, ambition, drive to overcome.

The life line is discussed in further detail in chapter 9, *Your Hand and Health.*

THE INNER LIFE LINE

This line (also known as a 'sister line') provides added strength and protection to the life line. It increases vitality and lends support (either physical or psychological) in the event of an accident, health problem, or other difficulty.

THE HEART LINE

The upper transverse line or *heart line* is our emotional barometer of life. Moving from beneath the Mercury finger across the palm, it reveals the quality of our emotions, our degree of sensitivity, and our capacity for love and affection. This line can also provide important information regarding the physical condition of the heart as well as the strength and type of our sexual desire.

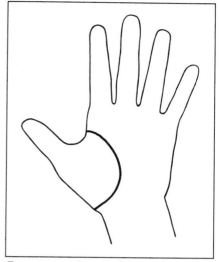

Figure 5.14: Long, clear and well-marked life line.

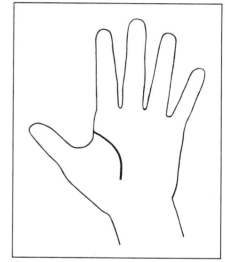

Figure 5.15: Short, clear and well-marked life line.

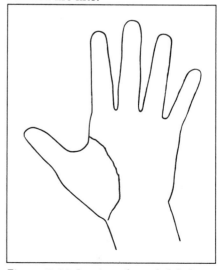

Figure 5.16: Long and weak life line.

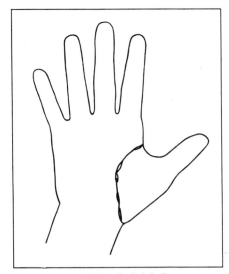

Figure 5.17: 'Islanded' life line.

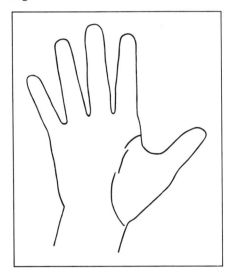

Figure 5.18: 'Broken' life line.

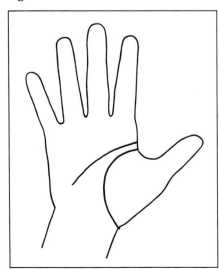

Figure 5.19: Life line separated from head line.

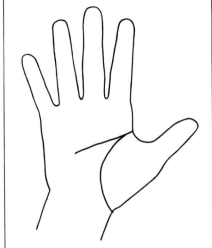

Figure 5.20: Life line connected to head line.

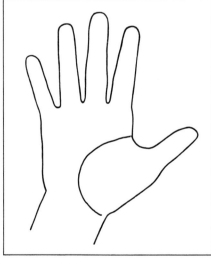

Figure 5.21: Life line forming broad arc around Venus mount.

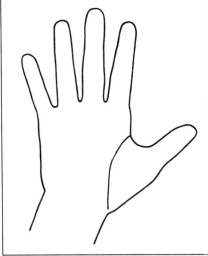

Figure 5.22: Life line hugging close to thumb, cutting into Venus mount.

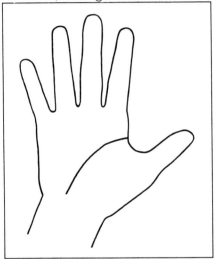

Figure 5.23: Life line moving towards mount of Luna.

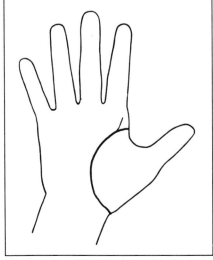

Figure 5.24: Branch from life line moving upwards towards Jupiter.

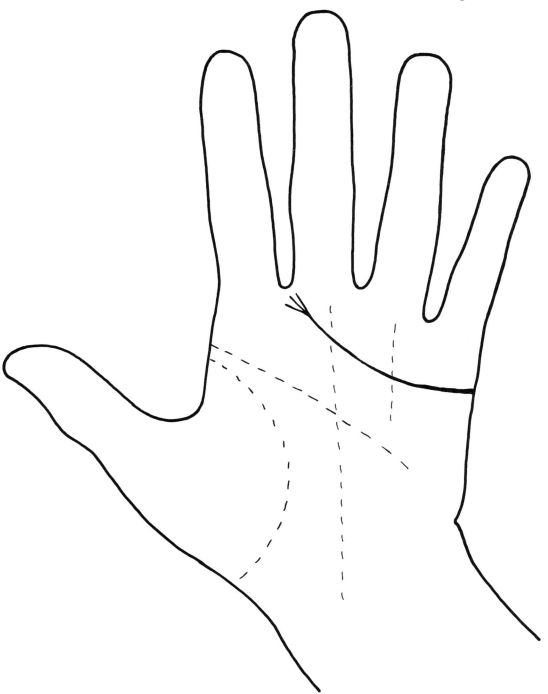

Figure 5.25: The 'ideal' heart line.

The 'ideal' heart line (Figure 5.25) is smooth, of good colour, and relatively free from islands and breaks. It would curve upwards slightly and end between the Saturn and Jupiter fingers, indicating a balance between the mind and the emotions. Two or three small branches would appear at its end, revealing a balance between sentiment, common sense and physical passion.

Figure 5.26: A straight, chained
heart line.

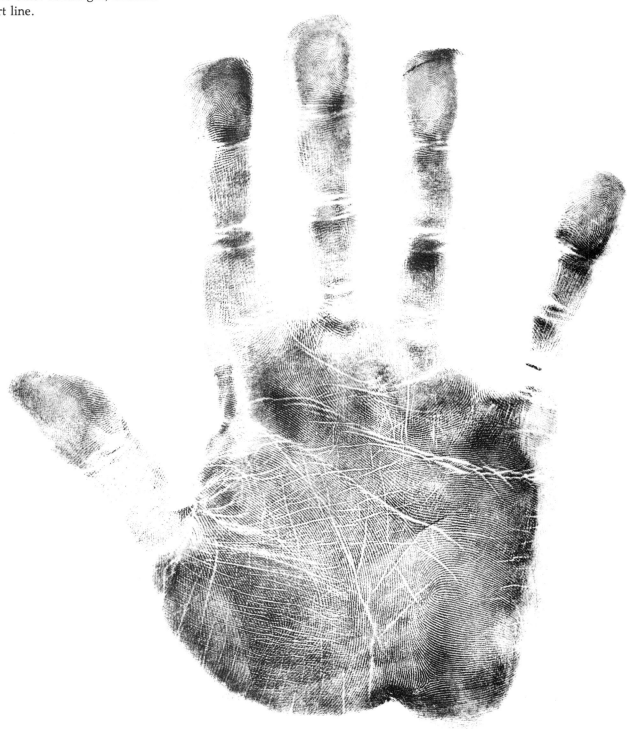

A straight heart line (Figure 5.26) reveals a more mental type of lover.
Fantasies, images and romance are important aspects of their sexuality,
which is primarily receptive in nature. When the line curves upwards
(Figure 5.27) a more physical, or instinctual sexuality dominates.

Figure 5.27: Heart line curving upwards.

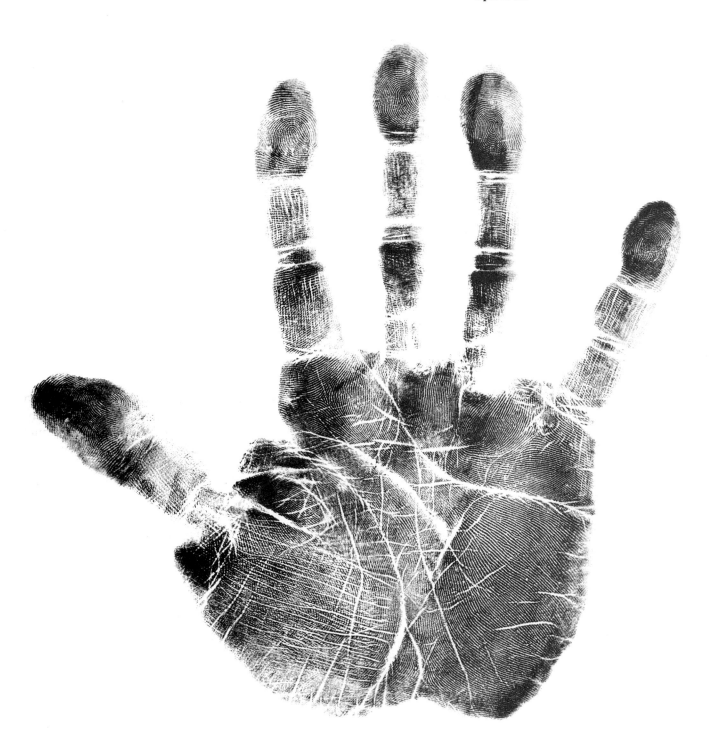

The major line characteristics include the following:

Ending under Saturn (Figure 5.28): Predominantly a physical type of sexuality; run more by the head than the heart in love relationships; can

Ending between Saturn and Jupiter (Figure 5.29): Balance between reason and emotions; warm hearted, generous, sympathetic.

Ending under Jupiter (Figure 5.30): Idealistic; ruled more by the heart than the head; more mental and emotional type of sex urges; a more romantic, poetic type of love.

Dropping to the life and head lines (Figure 5.31): Strong conflict between the heart and the head; powerful emotional feelings; easier to love humanity' rather than individuals.

Chained heart line (Figure 5.26): High degree of sensitivity; easily hurt and impressed by others. Desire for intimate contact, with accompanying fear of commitment. Tendency to be promiscuous.

Branches: Receptive nature.

Dots: Possible heart disease. See chapter 9 for further discussion.

Line joining heart line with head line (Figure 5.32): Balance between emotions and intellect in relationships.

Wide space between lines of heart and head (Figure 5.33): Broadminded, unconventional type of mental outlook. Impulsive and impatient, especially if the life and head lines are separate.

Narrow space between heart and head lines (Figure 5.34): Tendency to be narrow-minded and secretive. Repressed personality.

THE GIRDLE OF VENUS

The girdle of Venus is like a second heart line, and is located between the heart line and the top of the palm. Found on perhaps ten per cent of the population, its presence indicates sensitivity and emotional responsiveness. To the degree that it is clear and well-defined, the more balanced and properly channelled these emotions will be.

Altruism, compassion and sexual responsiveness are strong attributes of a girdle of Venus. However, if the girdle is broken and poorly defined (Figure 5.35) the person can be promiscuous, moody and self-indulgent. Examine the entire hand before arriving at such conclusions, however.

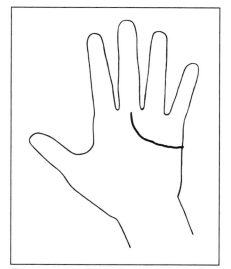

Figure 5.28: Heart line ending under Saturn.

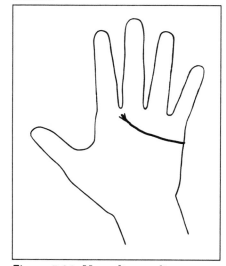

Figure 5.29: Heart line ending between Saturn and Jupiter.

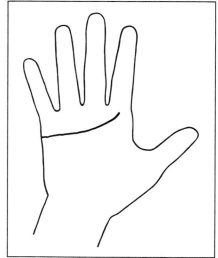

Figure 5.30: Heart line ending under Jupiter.

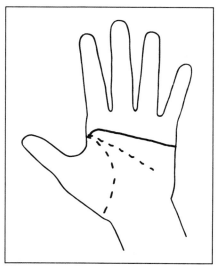

Figure 5.31: Heart line dropping to the head and life lines.

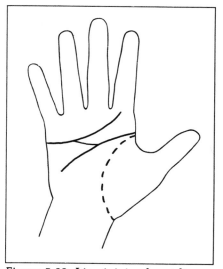

Figure 5.32: Line joining heart line with head line.

52

THE HEAD LINE

The lower transverse or *head line* begins at the line of life and moves horizontally across the hand. It reveals our intelligence, mental capacity and psychological disposition. The head line also records periods of emotional difficulty, mental illness and any accidents or illnesses which affect the head.

A 'good' head line is long, clear and free of islands, dots and breaks. It should slope gently downward and end with a small fork, denoting a balance between realism and imagination.

The major characteristics of the head line include the following:

Long (Figure 5.36): Intelligent, mental and emotional flexibility, wide range of intellectual interests.

Short (just reaching the Saturn finger) (Figure 5.37): Thought processes are limited primarily to mundane affairs.

Strong (Figure 5.38): Good mental ability and focus. Ability to concentrate.

Weak (Figure 5.39): Scattered intellect. Emotional difficulties, poor concentration.

Islanded (Figure 5.40): Difficulty in concentration; worry; psychological disturbances.

Wavy (Figure 5.41): Vacillation.

Moving straight across the hand (Figure 5.42): Practical, realistic, analytical.

Sloping slightly downwards towards Luna (Figure 5.43): Good imagination, creative intellect.

Dropping strongly towards Luna (Figure 5.44): Very strong and fertile imagination; tendency to live in a dream world. If line is broken as well, possible suicidal fantasies.

THE SIMIAN LINE

The so-called Simian line exists when both the heart and head lines join together as one. It appears as a straight line across the hand, as shown in Figure 5.45.

The Simian line tends to intensify both the mind and the personality. The individual often alternates between one emotional extreme and the

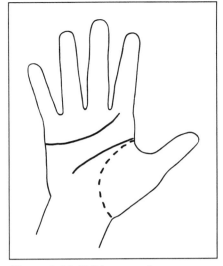

Figure 5.33: Wide space between lines of heart and head.

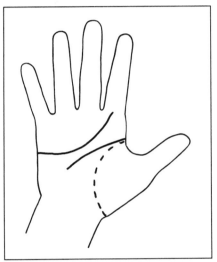

Figure 5.34: Narrow space between heart and head lines.

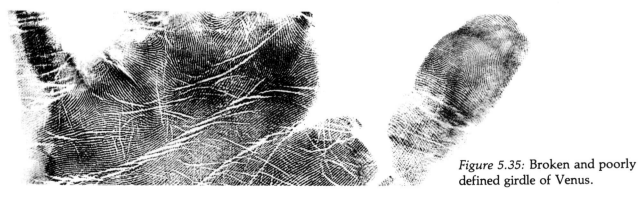

Figure 5.35: Broken and poorly defined girdle of Venus.

53

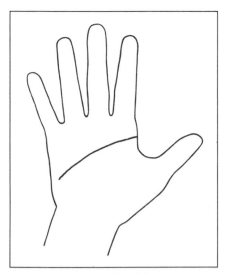

Figure 5.36: Long head line.

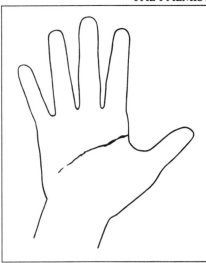

Figure 5.39: Weak head line.

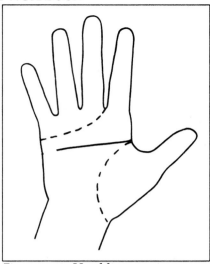

Figure 5.42: Head line moving straight across the hand.

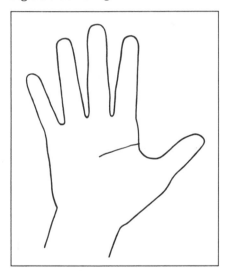

Figure 5.37: Short head line.

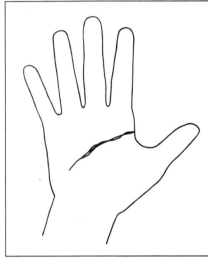

Figure 5.40: 'Islanded' head line.

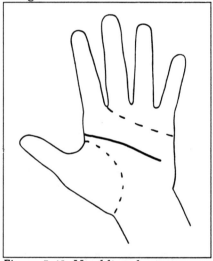

Figure 5.43: Head line sloping slightly downwards towards Luna.

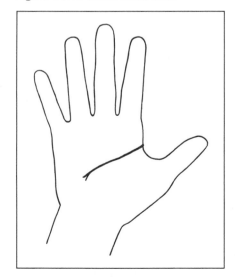

Figure 5.38: Strong head line.

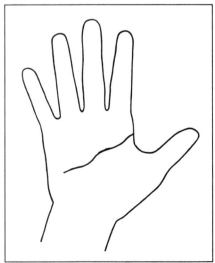

Figure 5.41: Wavy head line.

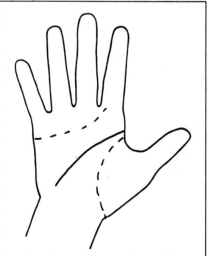

Figure 5.44: Head line dropping strongly towards Luna.

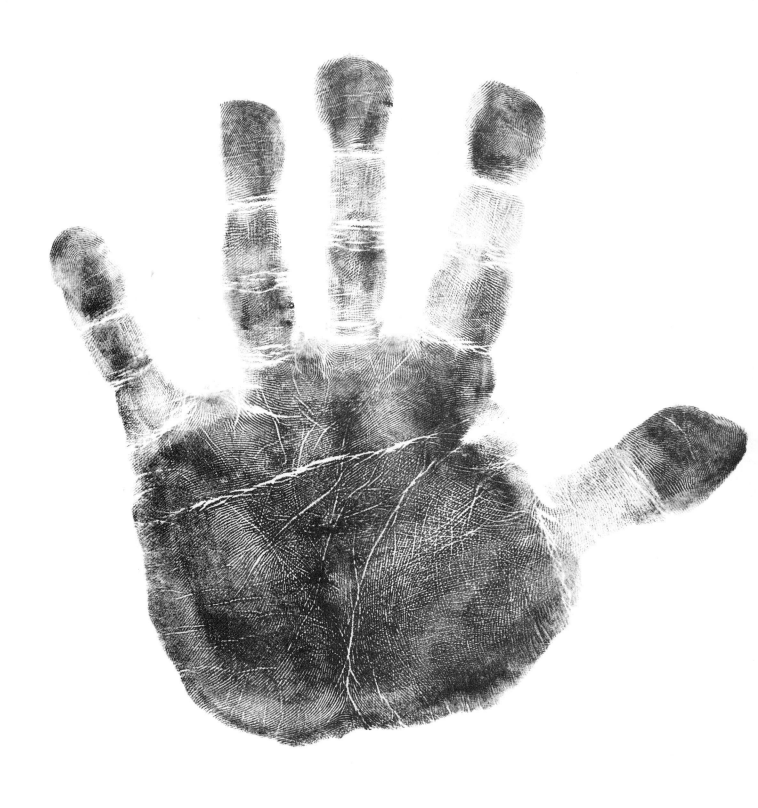

other, with the feelings often in conflict with the intellect. Those who possess this line have great tenacity of purpose and a strong capacity for accomplishment. If the mounts and fingers indicate a coarse personality, the owner of the Simian line can be violent and unpredictable. Be sure to examine the entire hand carefully before making your evaluation.

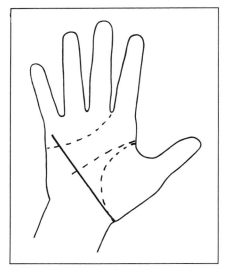

Figure 5.46: Deep line of Mercury, free from breaks.

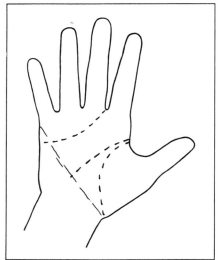

Figure 5.47: Breaks in the line of Mercury.

THE LINE OF SATURN

The line of Saturn (also known as the fate line, destiny line, career line, or line of life task) normally moves upwards from just above the wrist towards the mount of Saturn. More properly called the line of achievement' this line shows the degree to which we have fulfilled our deepest goals in life. It indicates our level of personal success and self-fulfilment as well as recording the obstacles, changes and restrictions which challenge us during our life.

It should be remembered that the implications of this line are highly subjective. A bank president who is frustrated with his profession can have a weak or broken Saturn line, while the man who cleans the executive's office and is very satisfied with his work can have a line that is strong and clear.

The Saturn line should be clear, deep and free of islands, downward branches and dots. The further up on the hand it begins, the later in life the person finds his life's work. Consult chapter 11 for a more detailed analysis of this important line.

THE LINE OF APOLLO

This vertical line, when it appears, is found under the mount of Apollo. Called the 'line of capability' by the American chirologist William G. Benham, the presence of this line indicates the potential of great achievement in life. It points to honours, success, money, and creative brilliance, especially in areas involving art and music. Many well-known artists, musicians, actors and writers have a strong line of Apollo, although this line is also found on people who simply love music, art and things of beauty.

THE LINE OF MERCURY

Known also as the health line or stomach line, the line of Mercury indicates the degree of balance in the physical organism and its basic nervous state.

Ideally, this line should not appear at all, but when it does, it moves from the base of the life line towards the Mercury finger. When deep and free from breaks (Figure 5.46) this line indicates a strong physical constitution and good digestion. Breaks in the line (Figure 5.47) reveal stomach and intestinal problems due to nervousness, repressed emotions, or strictly physical factors like poor diet or intestinal parasites. It may also indicate gynaecological problems in women.

TRAVEL LINES

Travel lines are small horizontal lines located on the outer edge of the palm and move up — according to the time of the trip in relation to the person's age — along the mounts of Luna and Mars towards the heart line. Each line represents an important journey. The trip may be important in terms of distance, duration, or its overall impact on the life of the person involved. For a diplomat who is constantly travelling all over the world, a month-long visit to the Far East would probably be of minor importance, while a two hundred mile journey for a farmer or invalid would appear on the hand as a major travel experience. The more important the journey, the longer and deeper the line.

Some people have a line which at first closely resembles a travel line, but it is located only on the mount of Luna and is deeper and longer. Although hand readers do not generally agree on its significance, this line appears to be found on people who are extremely fond of adventure and risk, whether physical, psychological or both.

LINES OF UNION

These small horizontal lines are found on the mount of Mercury and run from the percussion of the hand towards the inside of the palm. Often called 'marriage lines', the lines of union indicate important relationships which impress the person deeply. These relationships do not necessarily involve marriage. They can be with a man or a woman, and may or may not involve sex. The stronger the line, the deeper the potential union.

To determine age, measure upwards from the heart line. Midway between the heart line and the base of the Mercury finger should be approximately thirty-five years of age. However, rely on your intuition to determine the exact age.

CHILDREN'S LINES

The location of so-called 'children's lines' is subject to controversy among hand readers. From our experience, they appear as tiny horizontal lines located beneath the lines of union. Like other aspects of the hand, these lines reveal *potential* only.

In places like Latin America where contraception and abortion are still relatively uncommon, the indication of children on the hand is fairly accurate. Six children would be represented by six tiny lines under the line of union. In Great Britain, Europe, North America, and other industrialized regions, predicting the number of children is more difficult. Miscarriages and abortions would be recorded as potential children, as well as contraception by artificial means. In general, children's lines can be read with greater accuracy on the hands of women, although they may also exist on the hands of men.

THE LINE OF URANUS

The line of Uranus or the *intuitive crescent* begins on the mount of Luna and moves in a gentle arc towards the mount of Mercury, sometimes moving parallel to the Mercury or stomach line.

While this line rarely exists, it indicates powerful intuition with strong psychic abilities. It is often found on clairvoyants, mediums and healers. This line is more common in its incomplete state, and appears as a short line moving up from Luna towards the centre of the palm. It indicates intuitive perception.

Figure 5.48: The minor lines.

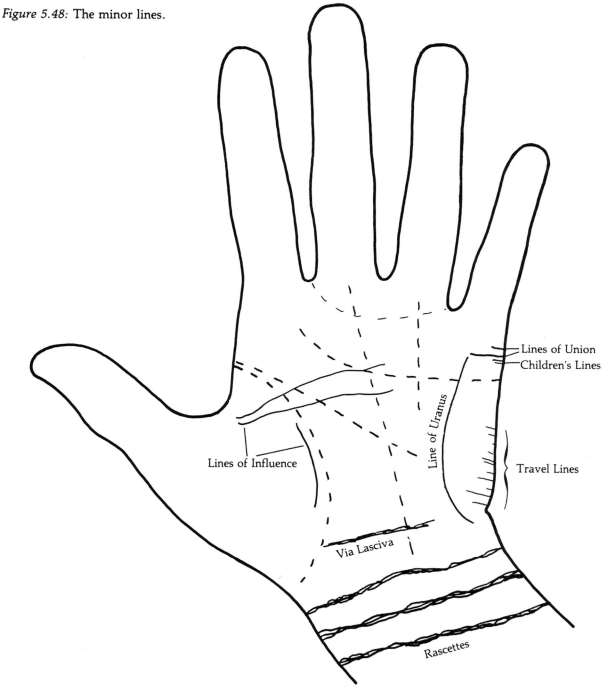

Lines of Union

Children's Lines

Line of Uranus

Travel Lines

Lines of Influence

Via Lasciva

Rascettes

THE LINE OF NEPTUNE

The line of Neptune, or *via lasciva* is also relatively rare. It branches off the life line and moves towards the lower mount of Mars or the mount of Luna, and is often weak and broken. The existence of this line reveals a strong sensitivity to drugs, alcohol, tobacco and other toxic substances.

RASCETTES OF VENUS

The rascettes are lines which appear on the underside of the wrist. Each strong, unbroken line is said to represent thirty years of good health. Weak, broken and chained rascettes reveal a weak physical condition, and have been linked to gynaecological problems in women. Be sure to examine other aspects of the hand for confirmation.

LINES OF INFLUENCE

Lines which run parallel to the vertical lines (such as those of life, Saturn and Apollo) strengthen these lines. In many cases, they repair a split or strengthen a section of a line that is islanded or chained.

Lines of influence also emanate from the mount of Venus and move horizontally across the hand, as shown in Figure 5.48. Generally speaking, they indicate obstacles, traumas and times of testing. They are not necessarily negative in meaning, and often record events which provide wisdom and life experience.

If, at the point of crossing a line (usually the life and/or head lines) a red dot is formed, a major illness or accident is possible. This would also hold true if an island or break follows the point of crossing. Examine other lines for confirming or modifying indicators.

By now you have a grounding in the basics of hand analysis. In the following sections, we will explore the deeper psychological aspects of chirology in detail. We will learn how the hands can help us stay healthy, enjoy greater fulfilment in our relationships, and achieve success and satisfaction in our career and spiritual life.

SECTION II
YOUR HAND AND
YOUR INNER WORLD

The following section provides a more comprehensive and integrated view of hand characteristics as they relate to the three major aspects of personality analysis: intellect, sexuality and will.

Unlike the previous chapters which offer a foundation for the interpretation of the various fingers, mounts and lines, the chapters which follow incorporate these aspects together into a unified, in-depth approach to character analysis and self-understanding.

Chapter 6

INTELLECT, IMAGINATION AND IDEATION

Perhaps the most outstanding feature of hand analysis is its ability to offer an objective and deep understanding of our intellectual state, including intelligence, memory and creative imagination. Unlike modern aptitude tests which measure only present ability (determined in part by social factors, education and 'test experience') the hand can reveal both present ability (by locating our age on the head line) and innate potential (by studying the head line and other aspects of the hand together). For these reasons, hand analysis can help us become more aware of our intellectual potential and explore ways to tap our inherent mental resources to realize our talents to the fullest.

YOUR HAND READING IQ

Intelligence works on both concrete and abstract levels, and involves a variety of factors: verbal comprehension and expression, the capacity to see similarities and differences between objects and issues, the ability to work with numbers and to compute data, and the capacity to find an underlying rule or structure in a series of events, objects or numbers.

Memory is another primary component of intelligence. It involves not only our ability to recall smells, visual impressions and memory related to touch, hearing or taste, but includes memories of people, places, events and other concrete facts dating back to earliest childhood.

The head line, as pointed out in the previous chapter, is our primary indicator of intelligence. Other factors, including the shape of the hand, as well as consistency and motility, can reveal the direction and the intensity in which these intellectual capacities can be expressed.

Basically, the head line shows both the level of our intelligence, and how well it is focused and integrated in daily life. This line should be clear, deep and free from islands, breaks and dots from beginning to end.

The longer the head line the greater the intellectual potential. An average head line extends to under the Apollo finger, while longer lines normally extend to the base of Mercury. Albert Einstein's head line is said to have run clear across his palm. A similar head line, reproduced in Figure 6.1, belongs to a woman who scored second in a series of

Figure 6.1: Hand print showing long, clear head line.

intelligence tests given to 2800 pre-university students by the New York City Department of Education, placing her in a 99.9 percentile.

Before we gloat or despair (as the case may be) over the length of our head line, it is important to remember that on the average, we utilize only *five to seven per cent* of our intelligence during our lifetime. So an individual whose head line barely clears the space under his Saturn mount may be using quantitatively more intelligence than his neighbour whose head line crosses the entire palm. The extent to which we use our inherent talents and abilities depends on us.

The clarity and strength of the head line are reliable indicators of present capability. A well-defined and clear head line — like the one just observed — reveals a good ability to evaluate concepts and situations, a strong memory, and a clarity of purpose that can lead to concrete action. Head lines which are chained, islanded or fretted, as seen in Figure 6.2, reveal a less 'grounded' type of mental energy which undermines clear

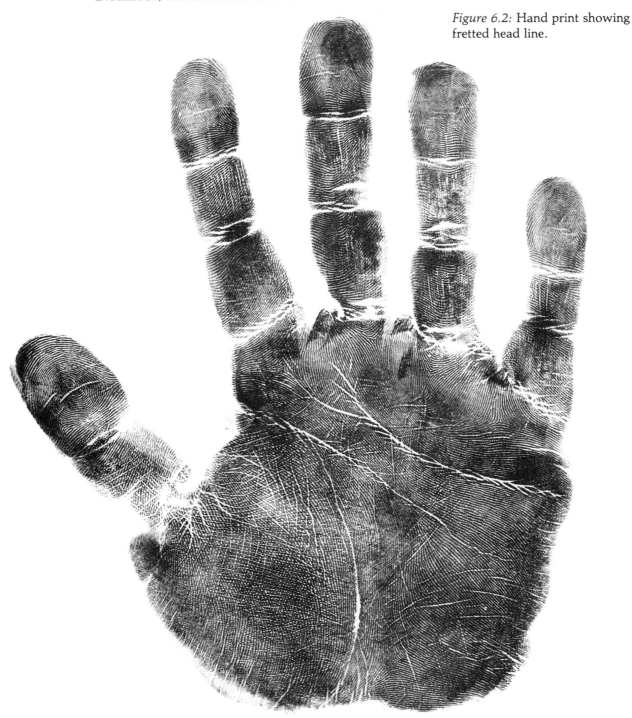

Figure 6.2: Hand print showing fretted head line.

thinking and diminishes our capacity to focus and act.

Islands have several meanings on the head line. They indicate difficulty in concentration, confusion, and a tendency to be 'scatterbrained'. Neurotic behaviour, such as anxiety, phobias or depression may also be indicated. The existence of islands may also be related to the abuse of drugs or alcohol, being the cause, the result, or both. As a rule, the larger the island, the more serious the mental or emotional difficulty.

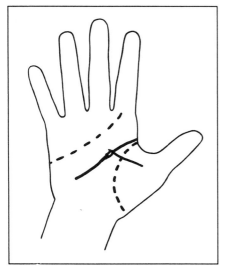

Figure 6.3: Island caused by influence line from mount of Venus cutting head line.

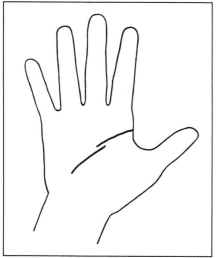

Figure 6.4: Overlapping breaks on head line.

When an island begins where an influence line from the Mars or Venus mount cuts the head line (Figure 6.3), chances are that a powerful trauma or other event set off a period of psychological difficulty. By the same token, an influence line may appear at the end of an island, indicating that the event or influence brought the period of difficulty to an end. When an influence line leaves a dot on the head line, the cause of mental or psychological weakness is physical in origin as the result of an accident or illness affecting the head directly.

Breaks on the head line indicate periods of transition. When lines overlap for a time (Figure 6.4) the changes would be more gradual, while a quick break (Figure 6.5) would be immediate, and possibly the result of an accident or other trauma. The quality of the head line at the point of breakage provides a good indication of how the person reacts to the transition. Often when we experience a period of difficulty we often view it in only its negative aspects, when in reality it may open the door to important perceptions and new opportunities. When a person goes through a difficult emotional transition, he needs to be guided to recognize the positive aspects of his dilemma and be encouraged to overcome his obstacles and move forward. Since the lines of the hand change (and breaks in the head line are especially known to mend) such encouragement can be a real service to the person seeking our help as hand analysts.

THE CREATIVE MIND

Creativity is closely related to intelligence, although it more reflects the personality. Creativity is primarily a measure of *divergent thinking* ('How many uses can you find for a kitchen knife?') rather than *convergent thinking* ('What is the capital of Nebraska?'). According to psychologists, factors related to creativity include unconventional thought processes, nonconformity, fluctuating moods, a strong intellect, and an interesting, arresting personality. Through careful study of the shape, texture and flexibility of the hand, along with an examination of the mounts, finger formation and finger spacing, we can have a good idea of the direction of a person's creativity and how it will be expressed.

Like intelligence, the primary measure of creativity is the head line. However, it is more the form of the line — rather than length alone — which determines how intellectual ability is applied, and whether the person's creativity is grounded or scattered.

Generally speaking, a head line which moves straight across the palm indicates an individual with a strong convergent mind. While he or she may know an abundance of information, there is a tendency to view the world primarily in practical terms. Imagination and creativity play a relatively minor role in life. People with this type of line like to follow rules and tend to dislike innovation. Their realistic, practical traits are often strengthened if their hands are rigid and are primarily of the square type.

A creative head line should slope gently downwards towards the mount of Luna, which indicates a balance between the realistic and imaginative thought processes. When the line ends in a small fork, this sense of balance is increased, and there is a union of practical and imaginative ideas with an ability to see both sides of an issue. When this branch is extremely long and wide (Figure 6.6), it indicates more of a split between these two worlds than a balance.

To the degree that the head line slopes towards Luna, the greater the divergent or imaginative thought processes. To learn whether or not the imagination is well grounded we must look to other aspects of the hand. Is the head line strong, or is it broken or chained? Does the flexibility of the hand show emotional stability? Does the space between the life and head lines show thinking before acting? Are the fingers conic, square, or mixed? Is the Saturn line strong or weak?

When the head line literally plunges towards Luna (Figure 6.7) the imagination is extremely strong. Islands or breaks in this type of head line indicate the possibility of the person 'going off the deep end' into a world of fantasy. If the space between the head and heart lines is narrow, the fantasy world is more secret and internalized. When coupled by a bent Saturn finger (indicating depressive tendencies) the strong feelings of depression and fantasy can result in suicidal thoughts. If a drooping head line contains islands or breaks towards the end, psychotic behaviour can become evident later in life. If the line is broken or fragmented (Figure 6.8) the person is often suicidal and should be referred to a competent professional for help.

This brings us to the subject of diagnosing mental illness in the hand. Several books, particularly *The Hands of Children* by Julius Speer and *The Hand in Psychological Diagnosis* by Dr Charlotte Wolff are devoted to the study of mental patients. Although both books were written decades ago, they are still valuable sources of reference for the professional therapist or serious student.

It is difficult to make specific psychological diagnoses from the hand. In the first place, it is well documented that normally rational and well-balanced people are capable of irrational, bizarre and even violent behaviour when placed in the appropriate conditions, especially during periods of extreme duress. In addition, people in history — including numerous composers, inventors and artists — who were condemned as 'mad' by their contemporaries have later been recognized as creative geniuses who did not conform to the accepted modes of behaviour of their age.

It is also important to avoid generalizations. Is a man who cuts his throat in a suicide attempt very different from another who commits suicide by eating the wrong foods even though his doctor advises him to abstain? Their hands may reveal different currents (the former's hand may include a classic 'suicide head line', while the latter's hand may appear completely normal). The end result, however, is the same. For this reason, we must consider the hand as a total unit, rather than make determinations from one or two aspects. In addition, we need to open our intuition to receive any subtle *energetic* messages the hand may offer us.

The hand reveals *potential*. We determine how this potential is expressed in life. A person with an abnormally long Jupiter finger, for example, can be dictatorial and overbearing. Another person with a similar characteristic can develop the positive aspects of Jupiter and become a revered spiritual leader known for his ability to inspire and teach.

However, there are several major indicators which can show the

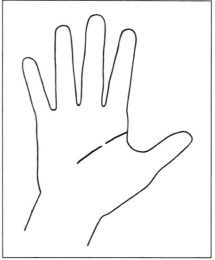

Figure 6.5: Quick break on head line.

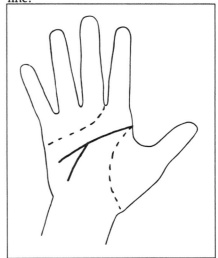

Figure 6.6: Head line ending in long, wide fork.

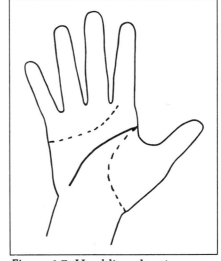

Figure 6.7: Head line plunging towards Luna.

Figure 6.8: Hand print showing fragmented head line.

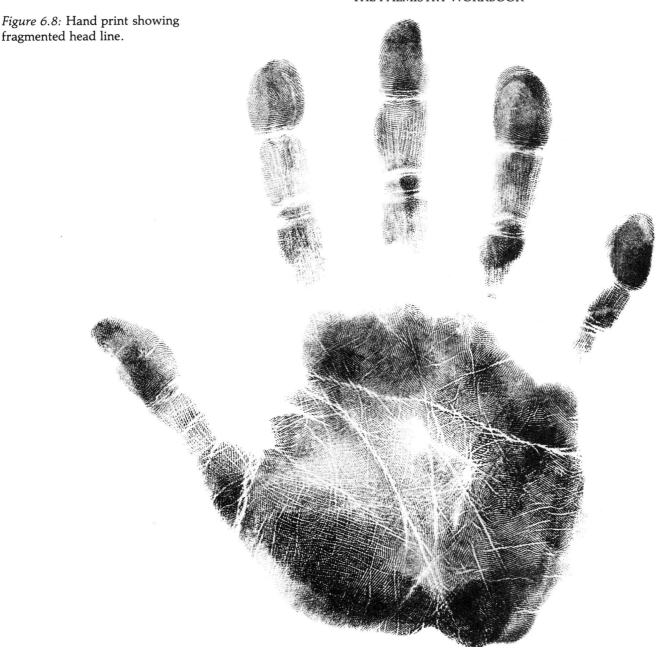

potential for mental illness on the hand. They represent extreme distortions of the basic 'core qualities' which the lines, fingers and other hand characteristics represent.

1. Hands and fingers which are abnormally small or large when compared to the individual's body size.
2. The Jupiter and Saturn fingers being of equal length, or the Saturn and Apollo fingers being of equal length. Dr Wolff found that such configurations appear primarily among schizophrenic patients.
3. Any finger which is abnormally short in comparison to the rest (such as a Jupiter finger which does not reach the top phalange of Saturn).
4. Fingers that are severely twisted or deformed (especially the Mercury

finger) when not the result of arthritis or accident.

5. Severely chained, broken and islanded head lines.

6. Head lines that are missing (especially in both hands) or extremely weak.

7. Hands, fingers and/or fingertips that are extremely rigid or hyperflexible.

8. A thumb that is abnormally short, deformed or placed extremely high on the hand to the extent that it appears similar to that of an infant.

9. A Simian line found on a poorly-shaped hand, or on a hand featuring one or more of the characteristics listed above.

It should be remembered that the existence of one or two of these traits does not mean that the individual is mentally ill. As mentioned before, the features of the hand reveal *potential*, which is always subject to change. In addition, modifying factors in the hand have been known to counteract negative qualities found in the hand shape, fingers and lines.

Whenever we find signs of difficulty on the hand, it is important to remember that apparent difficulties often open the door to opportunities which lead to transformation and self-realization. M. K. Gandhi became aware of his cruelty and violence during his teenage years. By learning how to transmute the energy behind his violent currents into positive directions, Gandhi was able to transform his life and change the destiny of his country.

When we have the opportunity to counsel others through hand analysis, we have a responsibility to help them get in touch with their reality. At the same time, we must couple this self-awareness with inspiration and constructive advice to help them take the next step. By learning how to contact the deepest essence of those who seek our help, we can serve as an effective catalyst for helping them realize their true potential.

Chapter 7

LOVE, RELATIONSHIP AND SEXUALITY

Perhaps the most deeply felt dissatisfaction in our culture is the ungroundedness of our sexual lives and the difficulty in establishing deep and satisfying romantic relationships with others. Although we may have more material knowledge about the philosophy of sex and sexual technique than ever before in history, many of us are ignorant of our overall psychosexual make-up and are not in touch with our real affectional and sexual needs.

Relationships are essential for both spiritual progress and psychological well-being. While we all need — and deserve — time by ourselves, the quality and depth of our relationships with others is a mirror of our own state of being and thus can be a reliable guide to our degree of personal integration and fulfilment.

Hand analysis can be a useful tool towards achieving this goal of self-understanding and integration. The hands reveal our basic level of sexual energy, and how it can translate into passion, commitment and our ability to love. They show our capacity for feeling, and can reveal mental and emotional blocks that can inhibit its flow. The hands help us determine our level of compatability with another, and how we can establish a relationship built on understanding and trust. Finally, by revealing traits, trends and abilities we may not be fully conscious of, the hand can help us change what blocks us from achieving satisfying relationships, while enabling us to draw on many of our positive 'core qualities' we may have overlooked.

SEXUAL ENERGY

Albert Szent-Gyorgi, the Nobel prize-winning physiologist, said that it takes energy to move the wheels of life. In humans, this energy is provided by the metabolic processes of the body. This has to do partly with the food we eat, the air we breathe, and our own unique genetic make-up.

Both the thickness and consistency of the hand are primary indicators of the amount of sexual energy we have at our disposal. However, other factors — including the size of the mount of Venus and the depth of the primary lines — can strengthen or neutralize these basic characteristics. While thickness is somewhat determined by the individual's physique, a very flat and soft hand reveals a low sex drive. The individual would tend to tire easily, would lack warmth, and would more likely want to be 'given to' rather than to give. A person with thin hands often lacks the warmth of the heart so necessary to a deep relationship. If the hand is thin and hard, the person will be stubborn, inflexible and calculating. A strong withholding current would be a major identifying trait.

A thick hand reveals the opposite qualities: an abundance of warmth, energy and sensuality. When the hand is thick and soft, there is a love for food and drink in addition to sex. Setting limits on these pleasures can be difficult, and weight control is often a problem.

When the consistency of a thick hand is hard and inflexible, this tends to accentuate a stubborn, cold and unbending emotional quality. People with this kind of hand are often sexually aggressive, emotionally demanding, and very difficult to be with. They think mostly about their own pleasure.

Between these extremes, a thick hand with an elastic consistency reveals a warm and sensuous individual with an abundance of sexual energy. This type of person enjoys a balance between receiving and giving pleasure, and generally has a good potential for establishing and maintaining good relationships.

The hand of medium thickness — both in women and men — reflects an energetic and warm person. Like their attitude towards food and drink, their sexual keyword is *balance*. They often tend not to be celibate or disinterested in sex, yet sex would not normally occupy all (or even most) of their thoughts and energy.

THE MOUNTS

The mount of Venus is a primary indicator of passion and sex drive. It speaks of vitality, the capacity for friendship, and our ability to love.

Ideally, this mount should take up about one-third of the palmar surface, and should neither be too hard nor too bland. 'Nice and round' would best describe a good mount of Venus. It reflects vitality, warmth and energy while indicating a strong capacity to love and be loved.

If the mount is very large, there is often an excess of physical passion and sexuality. If the mount is hard in addition to being large, sexual aggressiveness, brutality and cruelty (especially if the mount is reddish in colour and the upper mount of Mars is pronounced) are present. Strong grilles on the mount of Venus accentuate physical passion and sexual interest.

A small, bland mount of Venus indicates a general lack of vitality and sexual power. Although the person may well have strong feelings of love and passion, they are not expressed primarily through sex and physical contact. If the life line cuts into the mount — rather than sweeping around in a wide arc — the person can often be cold and prudish. Sexual expression is not a priority in life.

SKIN TEXTURE AND SEX

The texture of the skin is another important factor in determining psychosexual make-up, and should play a major role in any careful hand analysis. Smooth, fine skin reveals a strong degree of sensitivity and impressionability. Sex and sexual relations are often elevated to a romantic, idealized level. The person is more likely to respond to imagery and fantasy in sexual situations, and can more easily be affected by the energy, thoughts and words of the partner.

Coarse hands reveal a less sensitive nature, and the person tends to respond more to purely physical drives and stimuli. The individual is more prone to lack tact and sensitivity in sexual situations, and may often not be receptive to the partner's needs. When a man has a thick hand with coarse skin texture and his potential mate has a hand which is primarily thin and fine, chances are good that their relationship will be neither sexually nor emotionally compatible.

Medium skin texture — especially when complemented with small pads on the fingertips — shows a high degree of sensitivity and a balance between the receptive and active principles. While open to impressions and responsive to the feelings and needs of their partner, individuals with medium skin texture can also assert themselves in a relationship in a healthy way.

The flexibility of the hand in general and the thumb in particular can also tell us much about the way we respond to others in relationships. As mentioned earlier, hard, inflexible hands which do not bend back reflect a stubborn, rigid personality. The person is set in their ways and has difficulty accepting new ideas and adapting to unfamiliar situations. When the thumb is stiff as well (as is usually the case) the individual tends to be both materially and emotionally stingy. On the positive side, however, a stiff thumb is an indication of reliability and stability in a relationship.

The more flexible the hand, the greater the ability to adapt. There is an increased capacity to be open to new ideas and to flow with new situations. People with flexible hands are often more amenable to sharing problems in a relationship and are more approachable and less defensive than people with stiff hands. They are frequently less predictable as well. When the thumb bends back easily, generosity — both with material objects and feelings — is strong.

People with extremely flexible hands — hands which easily bend back to a ninety-degree angle or more — can be very exciting in a relationship. They are known for their spontaneity, adaptability and generosity, and are often quite unpredictable. However, if the thumb is weak and supple as well, sentiments can easily shift and a committed monogamous relationship is often difficult to maintain.

THE FINGERS AND SEX

The angle that the thumb forms with the rest of the hand is a good indication of the existence or lack of sexual inhibition. Remember to compare both hands to determine whether the individual has become sexually more liberated with age, or if sexual inhibitions have increased over the years.

A high set thumb, opening at a forty-five-degree angle to the index finger, is the sign of a Victorian in sexual attitudes. The individual is overly careful, correct, and withdrawn, and is either embarassed about sexual matters or avoids them completely.

When the thumb is at a sixty degree angle, there is a greater degree of psychological openness. While the individual is more liberated than the Victorian, there is still much fear of letting go especially if the hand is stiff and the head and life lines are joined.

As the angle of the thumb position increases, there is a corresponding lack of sexual inhibition. When the angle of the thumb in its relation to the index finger passes ninety degrees, the individual is sexually integrated and self-accepting. Sexual repression and fear of experimentation is minimal. When there is a separation between the head and life lines as well, these people have strong feelings of independence and self-confidence, which carry over into their relationships.

In addition to the thumb, the other fingers of the hand can tell us much about the way we relate to others. If the fingers are slender and pointed at the tips, there is often a lack of restricted control over instinctive desires. If this trait is coupled with a supple thumb, there may be difficulties maintaining a love relationship with one person. Fingers that are more squared-off or rounded at the tip can indicate a more monogamous trend in relationships, but should not be seen as a guarantee of faithfulness. By the same token, a strong thumb points toward relationships which are stable and constant. However, one must consider all of the hand characteristics together before reaching conclusions.

Ideally, the Jupiter and Apollo fingers should be the same length, and measure approximately one-quarter inch (.6cm) shorter than the Saturn finger. Such a configuration indicates that there is a good level of self-esteem plus the ability to appreciate the 'give and take' aspects of a relationship. When the Jupiter finger is shorter than Apollo, there is often a lack of self-esteem, which can lead to self-denigration and not standing up for one's rights. This tendency can be modified by a separation between the life and head lines at their commencement.

When the Jupiter finger is longer, the individual tends to be prideful and vain, and often needs to be dominant in relationships with others. The psychological need for sexual conquests is common. When the life and head lines are connected, there is often a fear that 'If I'm not in charge, someone else will control me'. When the head and life lines are separate, there is more independence and impulsiveness. While the person may be domineering and wish to be in charge, this trait is not based on fear, but is merely an aspect of leadership ability.

It was pointed out earlier that a straight Jupiter finger displays the finest Jupitarian qualities: generosity, inspiration, leadership and warmth. To the degree that this finger bends towards Saturn, we have a person who is jealous and possessive. When the Mercury finger bends in as well, there can be a tendency to 'do whatever is necessary' in a relationship to have one's way.

When the Saturn finger bends slightly towards Apollo, the person loves solitude and often needs 'space' in a relationship. This shouldn't

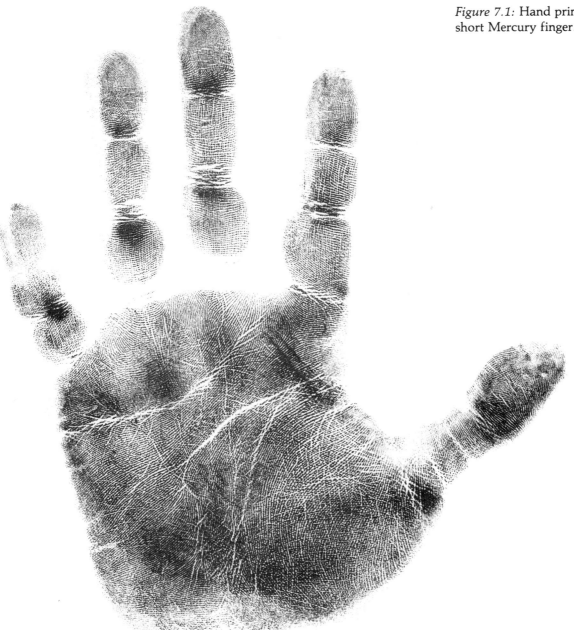

Figure 7.1: Hand print showing short Mercury finger.

be interpreted as being anti-social or withholding — the person merely has a need to spend time alone. If the finger bends sharply towards Apollo, however, the tendencies for melancholy and depression are strong. If the space between the head and heart lines is narrow, the individual can be secretive as well. People with such hands need to be with friends who are both understanding and trustworthy, and who can patiently help them slowly open up and share their problems and feelings.

When the Apollo finger bends towards Saturn, there is a tendency to place others on a pedestal and not see them as they really are. This can lead to disillusionment in a relationship, because these people expect more from others than can be realistically given.

A long Mercury finger highlights the ability to communicate and to relate well to others romantically. When this finger is short (reaching one-quarter inch (.6cm) below the joint between the second and top phalange of the Apollo finger) interpersonal communication can be difficult (Figure 7.1). When the finger bends inwards slightly, there is a tendency towards shrewdness and diplomacy. However, the more this finger bends towards Apollo, the greater the tendency to be manipulative and dishonest. A straight Mercury finger reveals a more honest individual, who often lacks diplomacy and shrewdness, except when a 'waisted' thumb is present. Very often this person is taken advantage of by others (usually by those with a sharply curving Mercury finger) and is frequently regarded as gullible and naïve. These qualities are accentuated in the rare cases where the Mercury finger actually bends outward, away from the hand.

NAILS

The nails are also helpful in determining character and how we relate to others. Long, broad and slightly rounded nails are a sign of openness, broad-mindedness, generosity, and a non-critical nature. Long, narrow nails — when not modified by other indicators on the hand — point towards suspicion, selfishness, and a tendency to be shrewd and calculating in relationships. Short nails reveal a critical individual who not only focuses on the perceived shortcomings of others, but is also very critical of himself. He or she often sabotages and downplays their own talents and positive character traits which instead deserve recognition and expression.

Nail colour is another expression of sexual vitality. Those with reddish nails tend to possess a strong sex drive and are more able to express this passion in purely physical terms. Bright pink nails tend to modify this powerful sex drive, and their owners tend to enjoy more of a balance between the physical and emotional expressions of love and passion. People with bluish nails often have difficulty expressing themselves physically. Although they may not lack passion and strong love feelings, it often takes them some time to 'warm up' to someone in a relationship.

THE LINES

Of all the lines in the hand, the *heart line* is the primary indicator of the way we feel towards others and how we relate to them. In addition to being our emotional barometer in life, the heart line reveals both the strength and type of our sexual expression.

As mentioned earlier, a good heart line is reasonably long, deep, smooth, and free of large islands or breaks. Such a line indicates strong feelings of affection, balanced by reliable and constant emotions. A person with this kind of heart line tends to feel secure in love and is devoted to their partner.

When the heart line is deep and chained, as seen in Figure 7.2, the person is very sensitive and often feels vulnerable in a relationship. There is a strong desire for intimate contact, yet an equally strong fear of

Figure 7.2: Hand print showing deep, chained heart line.

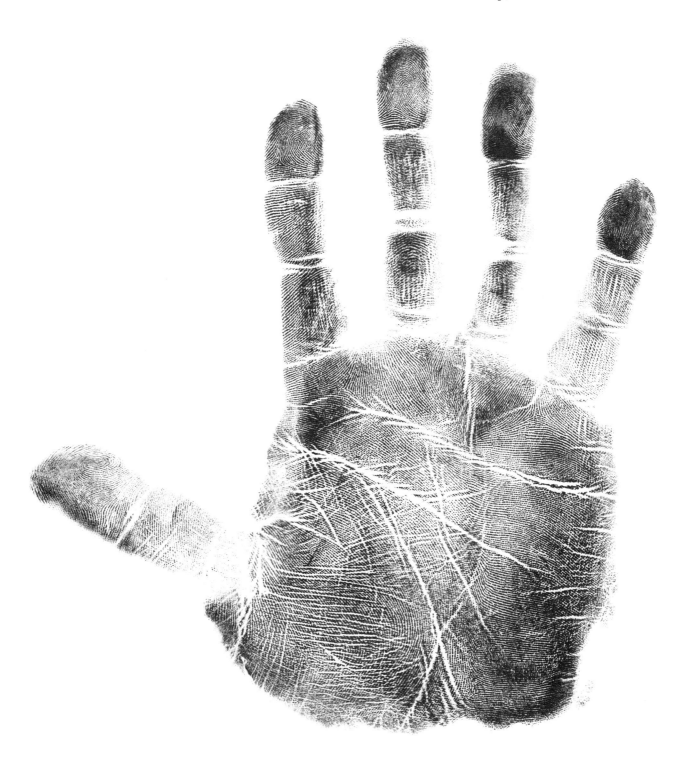

commitment. Such an individual needs to be honest with feelings and try to lower psychological defences. Otherwise, he or she can be taken for being aloof and disinterested, when in reality the opposite may be true. Chained and islanded heart lines also indicate inconsistency in feelings, with the emotions often confused and fragmented. When the heart line is wavy as well, these traits are often more pronounced.

A *straight heart line* moving horizontally across the palm reveals a basically sensitive and mental personality. Fantasies, romantic imagery and receptivity to emotional stimuli often predominate. This heart line is sometimes referred to as 'feminine' by palmists, because strong emotions and receptivity are considered feminine characteristics. However, this type of heart line is found on both women and men and should be more accurately termed a 'mental/receptive' heart line. People with this type of line — especially when it ends at or near the Jupiter mount — are more likely to be guided by romantic feelings that common sense, and are also more prone to be in love with humanity as a whole than to be romantically committed to a single individual. Examine the entire hand for possible modifiers.

A *curved heart line* moving up towards the top of the hand in a graceful arc is more physical than mental, and more assertive than receptive. A person with this type of heart line is more likely to be influenced by purely physical stimuli and instincts. Sexual expression will probably be more physical, active, and assertive.

The *length* of the heart line is also important. When the line ends under the mount of Saturn, the person may be quite physical, but on a deep level is ruled more by reason than by feelings. In general, sexual impulse is strong (especially if the mount of Venus is large and the heart line is 'physical' in character). If the heart line is strong and clear with a minimum of branches, the person may need to develop greater sensitivity to his or her partner's needs, although a small fork at the end of the line adds a degree of sensitivity to the personality.

A heart line ending between the mounts or fingers of Saturn and Jupiter are supposed to be 'ideal' because it shows a healthy balance between the heart and the head, or between reason and emotion. While the person would be warm-hearted, generous and sympathetic to others, there is also emotional balance and objectivity.

When the heart line ends under the Jupiter finger, the emotions tend to predominate over reason. Idealized love, sentimentality, and a strong degree of loyalty are common traits of those with this type of heart line. The tendency towards possessiveness and jealousy is often accentuated, especially if the Jupiter finger bends towards Saturn.

When the heart line moves clear across the palm and finally drops to touch the head and life lines (Figure 7.3) there is often a strong conflict between the heart and the head, which can lead to much suffering. If the heart line is chained (and it usually is) these people are very easily hurt, and have usually experienced a difficult childhood. They are often romantically attracted to numerous people and have trouble reconciling their universal affections with what society expects of them. These feelings are often intensified by the presence of a strong girdle of Venus. On the positive side, they are compassionate and sensitive to others, and can easily identify with those who suffer and who are in need. For this reason,

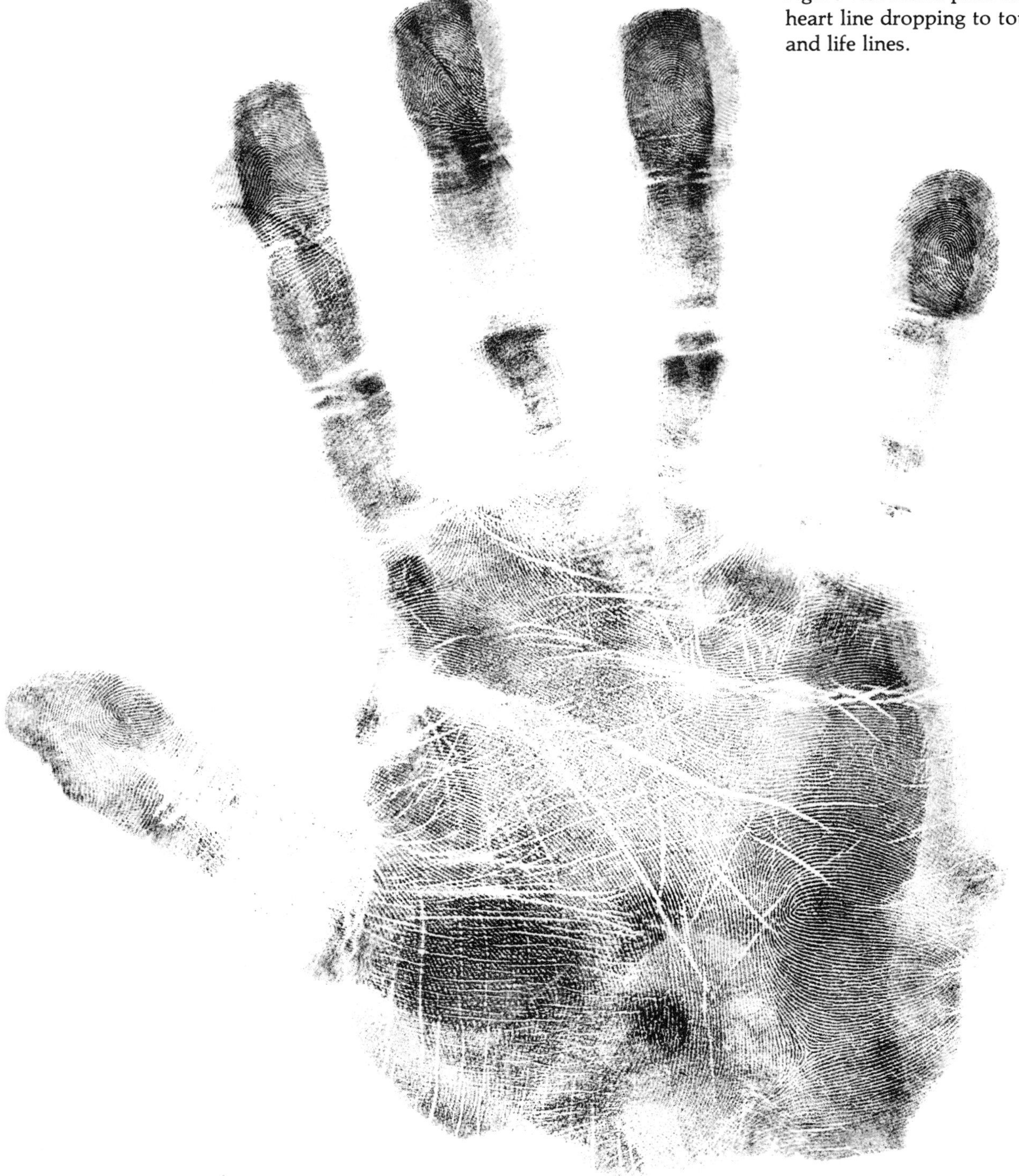

Figure 7.3: Hand print showing heart line dropping to touch head and life lines.

many people with this type of heart line make excellent doctors, teachers, therapists, ministers and others who like to help people.

A wide space between the heart and head lines indicates broadmindedness and an unconventional mental outlook, especially if there is a wide separation between the Apollo and Mercury fingers. A narrow space between the heart and head lines indicate a strong degree of secrecy and a feeling of not being 'at home' in the world. People with this formation often have difficulty expressing their feelings and are frequently self-conscious in social situations.

Branches at the end of the heart line add to the individual's sensitivity and receptivity. When the line ends in three short branches, there is a balance between sentiment, passion and common sense.

The direction of the *head line* also needs to be taken into account when considering sex and relationship in the hand. When the line moves directly across the palm, the person has a realistic view of love and relationship, and is often conventional, proper and practical where romance is concerned. The more the head line drops towards the mount of Luna, the greater the imagination and fantasy life. Since these qualities can be either positive or negative depending on the other character traits of the person involved, be sure to look for confirming or modifying factors in the hand (with special attention devoted to the fingers and their shape) before arriving at any conclusions.

The *girdle of Venus* indicates a strong level of emotional response. In general, those with a girdle of Venus are easily impressed by suggestion and sexual imagery, although the degree of response depends on the clarity, length and depth of the line itself in addition to the strength, direction and clarity of the head line.

THE HAND AND SEXUAL PREFERENCE

It is difficult to determine sexual preference from one or two aspects of the hand, because sexuality is an expression of the *whole person* and how he or she relates to life. Sexuality has its roots in our basic genetic make-up, our educational and cultural conditioning, and especially our primary relationships with our mother and father. Each sexual relationship mobilizes different aspects of this reality in us. For this reason, it is important to consider sexuality as part of the overall personality rather than as a separate part of one's life.

When it comes down to specifics, most books on palmistry either totally ignore the issues surrounding sexuality or discuss them with strong moralistic overtones. Given the seriousness of the subject — as well as the need of those who seek our help — we should approach issues of sexual expression with respect and sensitivity, free from critical and judgemental attitudes.

Masturbation

Years ago, masturbation was viewed with horror, and was said to be a primary cause of mental depression and insanity. Like public opinion of the day, many palmists felt that masturbation was sinful and reported that people who practised 'self-pollution' could be identified (to their shame) by a sweaty palm or a large red grille on the mount of Venus.

Although masturbation is seen in a more enlightened frame of reference, it still produces a good deal of misunderstanding. It should be of interest to the hand reader if sexual guilt — which stems primarily from old moralistic views — and repression seem to be a major problem for the person whose hands we are reading.

At the present time, psychologists consider masturbation to have several positive and even therapeutic aspects. It can be used as a way to discharge sexual energy and relieve tension when an appropriate sexual partner is not available. In addition, it can be used to bring us into deeper contact with our body and its sensations. Many women practise masturbation this way in order to later achieve more fulfilling relations with their partner. However, masturbation can also be used as an escape from relationships. It can be a problem when it is utilized purely as a compulsive act or as a way to avoid entering into a relationship with another person. The hand can reveal why this situation exists, especially through examination of the lines of heart, head and union, in addition to the mount of Venus and the girdle of Venus, if it exists. Through the insights gained into the total personality picture, we can carefully advise how such problems might be dealt with.

Same-sex orientation

The subject of homosexuality is a more serious issue, and nearly every book on palmistry has added to the confusion which exists regarding same-sex orientation. The hand of a homosexual — invariably a male — was portrayed as weak, with a supple thumb (revealing an unstable personality), a broken or islanded head line (indicating emotional problems), a long, chained heart line (showing that emotions rule over reason), a long, broken girdle of Venus (indicating sensitivity and strong sexual appetites) and pointy fingers (revealing artistic tendencies, capriciousness and lack of emotional balance). I have not found this to be the case at all (Figure 7.4).

It is very difficult — if not impossible — to determine sexual orientation from the hand. People with same-sex orientation are found in every culture and profession, and represent a wide spectrum of personality traits and human emotions. Psychologists have found that in almost every area but sexual expression, 'straight' and 'gay' people are identical. Some gay people have problems with self esteem while others do not; some are sensitive while others are not; some are socially well adjusted while others are not. While certain gay men enjoy flower arranging, some prefer rugby, while others like both flower arranging *and* rugby.

In many cases, the boundaries between homosexual, bisexual and heterosexual expression are quite vague, and blanket statements rarely serve a worthwhile purpose. The hand can, of course, provide insight into the person's sensitivity, emotional response, the degree of sexual repression operant in the personality, issues of aggressiveness and passivity, cruelty, the capacity for love and the ability to enjoy fulfilling relationships. Whether such feelings are directed primarily towards men or women (or both) is extremely difficult to assess. Of course, if you know or intuitively feel that the person you are reading for is gay or bisexual, your consultation can be guided accordingly. For example, instead of speaking of the woman or man they will marry, you can speak of a primary relationship without referring to gender.

Figure 7.4: Hand print of a successful 45-year-old gay man who has been involved with environmental organizations during much of his adult life.

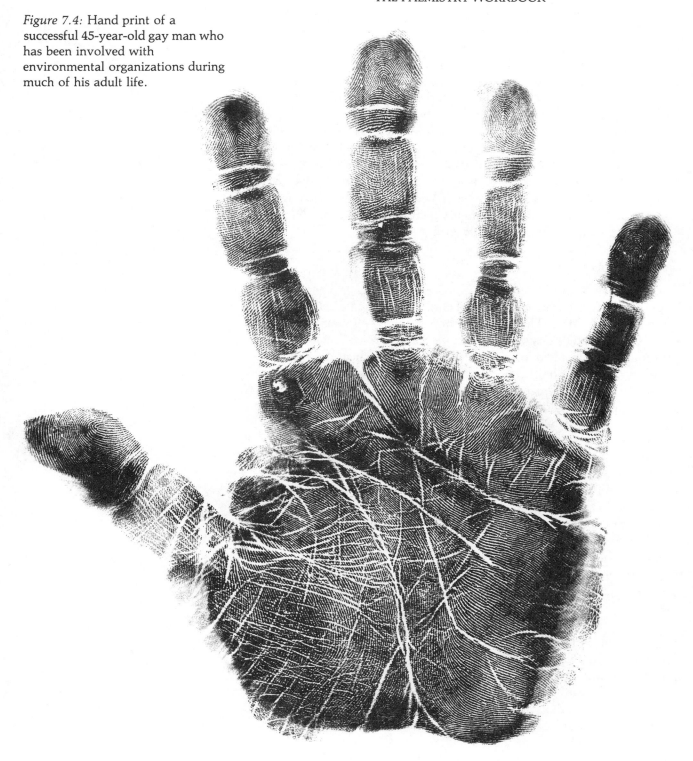

Other variations

Other avenues of sexual expression — including sado-masochism, incest, voyeurism, and fetishism — are often expressions of energetic blocks both on physical and psychological levels, and are difficult to determine by hand analysis alone. Like sexual preference, the boundary between having such inclinations and acting them out is often very fine. Psychologists tell us that nearly everyone has entertained thoughts of sadism, masochism, incest or voyeurism at one time or another, even though such feelings are rarely, if ever, expressed.

Stereotyping hands must be avoided. A 'sadist's hand' is supposed to be coarse, hard, and red in colour. We have been told that the mounts of Venus and Mars should be large and hard, and a 'Murderer's thumb' is often present. The problem is that there are people with such hands who are not sadists, while some people with fine hands, long slim fingers, and fine skin texture may act out their sadistic feelings every day of the week. Again, it is important to view the hand as a *totality* and be open to intuitive perceptions rather than arriving at stereotyped assumptions.

Impotence and fridigity

There are physical, energetic and psychological causes of impotence and frigidity. While there are no clear-cut indications of these sexual problems on the hand, one can observe several markings in the palm which may contribute to the problem. A small and weak mount of Venus, a thin hand of flabby consistency, a life line cutting through the mount of Venus, and a weak heart line can indicate that sexual expression is not a major priority in life.

However, other factors should be considered. While the hand markings mentioned above may reveal potential, the actual relationship between the two people involved is of primary importance. Before we consider an individual problem, we should see it in the light of that specific relationship and the conscious or unconscious energetic connection between the partners. In that relationship, the woman may be frigid or the man may be impotent. Different people react in different ways depending on their 'chemistry' together, negative past experiences, anger, or issues of guilt or sexual repression. Stress on the job or other external factors may also be involved. Remember to observe the problem in the context of the relationship. However, if the difficulty is chronic — meaning that the man has been impotent in his four previous relationships as well — it is more an individual problem and should be worked with accordingly.

Remember that people who are anxious, repressed or angry are not necessarily impotent or frigid, so general statements should be avoided. However, if sexual dysfunction is mentioned by the person as a problem, you can offer much worthwhile information regarding the primary issues which prevent him or her from enjoying a fulfilling relationship with another.

MARRIAGE IN THE HAND

The so-called 'marriage lines' of the hand are actually lines of union. They indicate the potential — and possible time — of an important relationship (or relationships) in a person's life. As we mentioned earlier, this union may be with a man or with a woman, and may or may not include sex.

In some cases — as in the hands of people in which the legal marriage is superficial or psychologically distant — the line of union can indicate a close friend with whom there is a primary (though not necessarily sexual) relationship.

For this reason it is difficult to be certain as to whether a line of union indicates a traditional marriage or not. As with understanding other major aspects of the hand, the reader's intuition can play a major role in evaluating the present and potential existence of a marriage-type relationship.

In general, the longer the line of union, the longer the relationship, and the deeper the line, the more important the relationship is in the person's life. Breaks or islands indicate problems in the relationship which can lead to its termination. When the union line drops slightly towards the end, it is believed that the person will probably outlive his or her mate.

Planning the future

One of the more exciting trends in palmistry is a compatability study of the hands of both partners to determine areas of harmony and conflict, as well as issues of jealousy, greed and domination.

While such a study is often very useful for the people involved, such a reading can more easily include the intrusion of the hand reader's feelings into the reading and hence the relationship itself. Because the reasons why two people establish a relationship may go beyond reasons of sex, pleasure or companionship (some people may have ancient 'karmic issues' which need to be worked out between them) we need to be extremely careful not to make any pronouncements relating to the advisability of their establishing or continuing the relationship. Very often a compatability reading can help prolong a relationship which should be ended, or can help kill a relationship which may need to run its course.

Reading for one person is a difficult task, but an in-depth reading for a couple is a highly sensitive matter. It is suggested that the hand reader possess a high level of expertise before becoming involved in such delicate work.

For further discussion, consult my book *Sexual Palmistry* (Aquarian Press, 1986).

Chapter 8

WILL: FROM INERTIA TO ACTION

Will is a divine aspect of the universe, and is a potent source of strength and power. It enables a plant to break through concrete as it grows, and gives many animal species their tenacious and often uncanny ability to adapt and flourish in a hostile environment.

In humans, will is connected with the soul, or 'the essence, substance, animating principle or actuating cause of life'. The will aspect stands behind our ability to survive, to grow, and to manifest our talents and abilities. Without will, humanity would not have been able to evolve. It is the power which helps us explore new horizons and to create cities, nations and civilizations.

On a psychological level, will is closely related to the ego, or our 'I-am-ship'. It is concerned with one's awareness of oneself as a distinct human being, capable of love, creativity and self-realization. In esoteric philosophy, it is taught that we possess two egos: the *mortal* or *personal* ego, which governs the basic needs and desires of the personality, and the *divine* ego, which represents the spirit, the 'Christ within' or the higher self.

On the most elementary level, will is closely connected with the mortal ego, and represents our basic instinct to survive. In addition to the will to live, we also exert will in order to achieve and maintain the family structure.

As expressed through the mortal ego, will is also involved in more complex psychological issues, including our need for pleasure, power, status and security. Will is often connected with issues of control, possessiveness, and domination in the family structure, especially with one's spouse and children. When expressed in the context of the workplace, will can manifest as greed, competition, or leadership. In a social environment, will can involve the struggle to obtain social benefits, such as status, popularity and respect.

As we become more mature on a personality level — and when soul energies transmute from lower levels to higher level of consciousness — the energy of will is changed to more reflect the divine ego. This level is more connected with feelings of inclusiveness, the application of inner wisdom, and the ability to be open to God's will. To the extent that the personal ego can work harmoniously with the higher self, the greater the degree of personal integration, inner peace, and self-fulfilment.

We can see the expression of will in the hand. It is primarily reflected by the strength, form and position of the thumb, the power of the mounts, and the clarity and shape of the major lines. By understanding our strengths and weaknesses — and transforming any negative currents into positive core qualities — we can harness the power of will and make it work for us.

Hands of the square, spatulate or mixed type often reflect a strong will, especially if they are firm, strong, and moderately pliable. Narrow, pale and overly-soft hands with weak or flexible fingers generally indicate emotional instability, lack of resolve, and difficulty in standing up to adversity.

THE THUMB: EGO INCARNATE

The thumb represents our individuality and the ability to assert ourselves in the world. On a purely physical level, the opposed thumb sets us apart from the other animals — including the apes — and gives us the ability to perform tasks — such as construction, mechanics and surgery — which

Figure 8.1: American composer Aaron Copland has a strong, expressive thumb.

no other species can accomplish. Without this type of thumb, our ability to communicate, repair, build, invent and create would be greatly diminished.

On a psychological level, the thumb represents the power of the ego, both on 'mortal' and 'divine' levels. It symbolizes the strength of our individuality, and our capacity to express our desires, aspirations and talents in daily life. We know that infants tend to hide their thumbs from the world until they reach a point in development when they feel more comfortable in their mean environment. Adults — going through periods of fear or extreme stress — often cover their thumbs with the other fingers in a regression to their protected lives as infants.

The more prominent the thumb, the greater the ego strength. A long, strong, firm and 'expressive' thumb reveals courage, stability and will-power. The fingertips add character and direction to the thumb. A spatulate tip, for example, reveals an individual of action, who likes to throw himself into business deals, creative projects, and all kinds of adventures. A square tip shows that the ego will probably express itself in organizational and administrative affairs, while a conic fingertip would favour one's artistic ability and the desire to create, whether it be a sculpture, a computer program, or a musical composition.

The strong rounded thumb of the American composer and conductor Aaron Copland (Figure 8.1) is a good example of how will plays an important role in creativity. In addition to the strength which the thumb imparts to his hands in general, the expressiveness of the thumb is especially present when the maestro conducts.

A short, thin and flat thumb generally reveals a lack of self-confidence and self-assertion. The individual tends to underestimate his or her talents and abilities and has difficulty overcoming adverse situations.

While a flexible thumb reveals adaptability, generosity and spontaneity, it can also be a sign of poor will power. People with flexible thumbs often have a difficult time sticking to a diet or attempting to adhere to a budget. However, a weak thumb can be strengthened by a firm hand, strong mounts of Mars and Venus, and a long prominent Jupiter finger.

In general, the longer the phalange of will, the greater the will power and the ability to put thoughts into practice. The phalanges of the thumb are discussed in greater detail in chapter 4.

The position of the thumb is also important. The further the thumb is held from the other four fingers, the greater the degree of courage, self-confidence and independence. Strong thumbs which separate from the hand (at an angle of sixty degrees or more) are found on many executives, military leaders and others who need to make important decisions and stand behind them. The low-set thumb of a twenty-two-year-old South American exile (Figure 8.2) who was involved in anti-government activity in college, reveals his commitment to political action, love of adventure, and his desire for independence.

Conversely, a high-set thumb located close to the rest of the hand reveals a more contracted personality who has difficulty standing up and asserting himself, especially if the thumb is also short, thin, or flat.

Figure 8.2: Hand print showing low-set thumb of an man committed to his political beliefs.

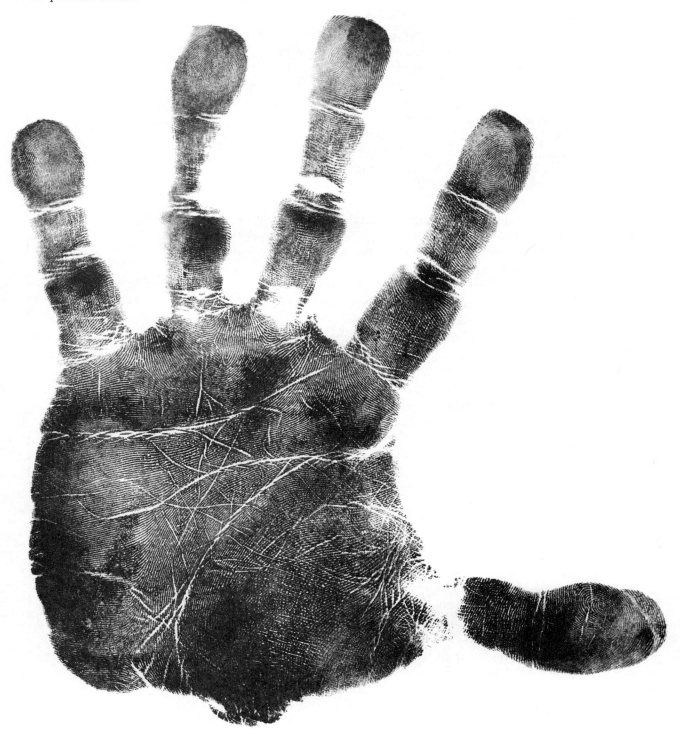

THE MODIFIERS

While the thumb is the principle indicator of ego strength and will power, other aspects of the hand can reveal important information which can modify the essential qualities which the thumb reveals.

A Jupiter finger that is longer than Apollo can strengthen the thumb. Egotism, optimism and the ability to lead and inspire (as functions of will) are several of the qualities indicated by a strong Jupiter finger.

When the head and life lines are separate, the power of Jupiter is increased. The individual has a greater ability to inspire, execute and act in a natural leadership role. When the lines are connected, a long Jupiter finger tends to indicate a need to dominate and control. The strong ego is eroded by lack of confidence, which is an expression of weak will. The message is 'I have to be boss, or someone else will dominate over me'. The person needs to be on top of a situation rather than be open to the natural flow and movement of life.

The mounts can also strengthen or detract from the qualities of a strong thumb. A strong Jupiter mount increases self-confidence and leadership ability, while a strong Saturn mount enhances emotional stability and thoroughness. A prominent mount of Upper Mars increases courage and resistance, especially when the individual is confronted by outside pressures. When this mount is weak or soft, the person has difficulty standing up for himself and can easily be controlled by others. A strong mount of Lower Mars (it often appears as a callus or 'tumour' on the palm) reveals aggression and strong temper. A prominent mount of Venus imparts more energy and power to the thumb, thus strengthening the ability to move forward and create.

Lines can be additional modifiers on the hand. Strong clear lines (as seen in Figure 8.3) help strengthen all aspects of the personality, including will. In regard to specific lines, a long and sensitive heart line, for example, reveals a highly compassionate nature, which can modify a firm, straight and 'stubborn' thumb. A clear, deep head line can add resolve to a weak thumb or index finger, and enhance our ability to translate thought into decisive action.

When evaluating a hand, it is important to offer a balanced view of an issue. We need to focus on the truth of what we see and, when appropriate, offer guidance to help the person whose hand we are reading resolve areas of weakness or difficulty. In addition, we should bear in mind that negative traits as revealed in the hand are often distortions of positive core qualities. A long Jupiter finger, for example, can reveal a dominating and controlling personality, but with awareness and resolve, can be transformed into an ability to inspire and to lead others to discover their own inner strengths and abilities. A stiff thumb may indicate stubborness and inflexibility, but also can reflect an inner stability which can be open to change. A high-set thumb may indicate fear and a reluctance to experience life, yet it can also reflect a healthy caution and a quiet sense of self-worth.

By dealing with issues of self-esteem and will with sensitivity and

Figure 8.3: Hand print showing clear, modifying lines.

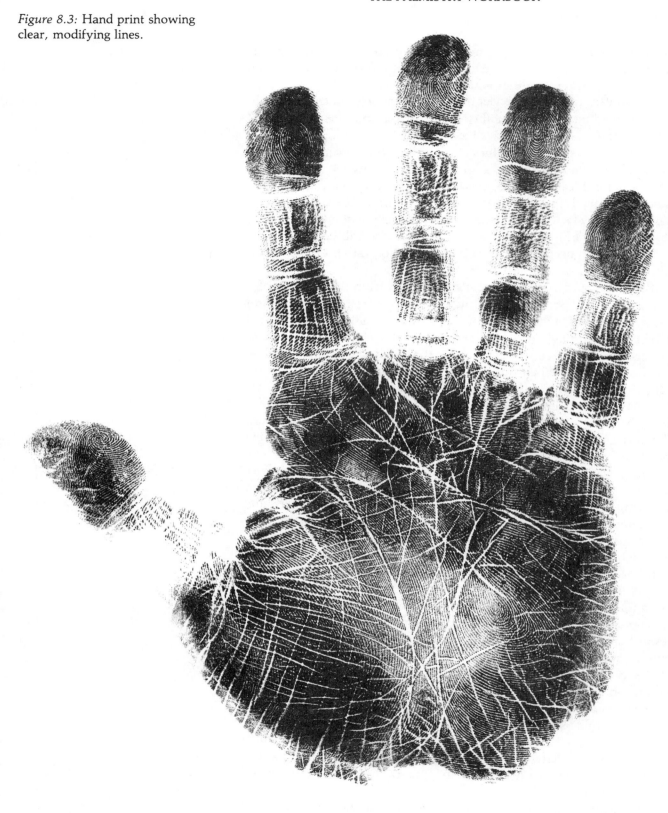

compassion, we open ourselves to intuitional perceptions which can truly help the person we are reading accept himself as he is, and work with areas which need attention and transformation according to his circumstances and abilities.

Section III:
Health, Life Task
and Spirituality

The previous three chapters were devoted to our inner psychological state as seen in the human hand. The following three chapters will explore how intellect, love and will can practically manifest in daily life. Although there are many possible areas of study, we will focus on those of health, spirituality and career .

Chapter 9

YOUR HAND AND HEALTH

Although thousands of years old, doctors have taken a new look at the ancient science of hand analysis as a guide towards understanding the dynamics of health and disease. While orthodox physicians have studied the colour of the nails and the temperature and texture of the skin for decades, an increasing number of doctors — like Eugene Scheimann, MD of the American Hospital in Chicago — feel that the texture, flexibility, colour, ridges and especially the lines of the human hand provide important guidance for the prevention, diagnosis and alleviation of disease.

WHAT IS HEALTH?

According to the World Health Organization of the United Nations (WHO), health is 'a state of full physical, psychological, and social well-being, not just the absence of disease or incapacity.' *Dorland's Medical Dictionary* agrees, and adds that health is a state or condition of wholeness, in which all body parts and functions are co-ordinating properly.

Our level of health is determined partly by heredity, but is mostly dependent on how we are able to adapt to our environment: fighting germs, dealing with stress, and resisting the threat of pollution or accident. Healthy diets, stress management, positive mental attitudes, rest, and regular exercise are major factors in achieving and maintaining good health. Since only unhealthy bodies provide fertile ground for disease in the first place, maintaining a healthy body should be one of our primary goals in life. From Hippocrates onwards, health practitioners have considered the hand a reliable indicator of heredity, emotional make-up and physical constitution. Today more than ever before, the hand can serve as a primary tool to help us understand our health picture and work towards achieving the level of well-being we deserve.

Hands show tendencies and not always definite facts, and the lines of the hand can change dramatically — sometimes within several weeks. Therefore, statements like 'Your life line says that you will die by age 40' or 'You will come down with cancer' are both fraudulent and irresponsible. The fact that you have a long life line is no guarantee that you won't be run over by a taxi on your way to work, or a sign indicating a tendency for cancer does not mean that you won't live a long, cancer-free life.

However, to the degree that you as a hand reader can recognize predispositions to certain health problems, chirology can be a valuable tool in both the prevention and cure of disease. In addition to providing important indicators to possible ill health, the structure, texture and lines of the hand offer hope to those of us who want to maintain their maximum health potential.

Your hand is like a complex puzzle that can change constantly. By understanding individual characteristics — like temperature, consistency or lines — and making both mental and intuitive connections regarding their relationship with each other, you can use the hand as an ongoing guide to insure your own good health and the well-being of those who seek your aid.

YOUR HAND: TEXTURE, TEMPERATURE AND COLOUR

Skin texture is a useful indicator of our inner nature. If the skin is soft and fine, it reflects both physical vulnerability vis-à-vis the environment. A coarser skin texture would indicate an individual whose health is not strongly influenced by external factors like temperature, noise and pollution.

Doctors have long known that dry, rough, scaly hands indicate an underactive thyroid gland, while very warm, oversmooth and satiny hands can be a sign of thyroid overactivity. Soft, pudgy fingers which take on the appearance of sausages may indicate thyroid problems as well.

If the person's hands are cold and clammy, he may be nervous (especially if his hand is being read for the first time). Find out if the anxiety is temporary or chronic, because clammy hands can also be an indication of insomnia. If the hands (especially the fingertips) are cold — even on a warm day — poor circulation may be present, especially if the nails take on a bluish tinge.

The normal colour of the palm is rosy and pinkish (regardless of race or skin colour) which testifies to good blood circulation and normal body functioning. *Extreme redness* indicates excessive blood circulation in the hands and can point to a tendency for high-blood pressure, diabetes, gout, heart disease or stroke. *Pallid skin* usually indicates a state of anxiety or anaemia. In his excellent book *A Doctor's Guide to Better Health Through Palmistry*, Dr Scheimann suggests that if you bend the hand back and the main crease lines are pale, an iron deficiency may be present.

Warm, bluish hands reveal poor blood circulation or possible heart disease, and have been linked to Reynaud's syndrome, atherosclerosis and certain adverse drug reactions. If the hands are cold and bluish, the circulatory problem is more localized. Consult a health professional for proper diagnosis and treatment.

Yellowish hands are relatively uncommon, but are a probable indicator of liver disease, including hepatitis and jaundice. However, before you reach such dire conclusions, find out about the person's diet. Yellowish hands are often found among those who drink large amounts of carrot juice.

CONSISTENCY AND HEALTH

The consistency of the hand is a valuable indicator of health, because it helps us determine the amount of energy we have at our disposal.

Flabby and soft hands lack muscle tone and are often small, broad and bland to the touch. People with flabby or very soft hands tend to over-indulge in life's pleasures, including food, alcohol and sex (especially if the hands are thick). They are often lazy and have difficulty sustaining will power, particularly if the thumb is flexible or weak. *Thin, flat and weak hands* reveal a lack of energy and difficulty sustaining long-term activity. People with these hands are very susceptible to disease and are more prone to vitamin deficiency than others.

Firm hands, which are more muscular, reveal an energetic, strong and active person who leads a more balanced life. While showing a high degree of responsibility and self-restraint, firm hands also characterize a person who can adapt to unexpected circumstances and be open to new and unfamiliar ideas. As a result, people with firm hands are more resistant to disease.

Hard or rigid hands do not bend under pressure. Unlike the firm hand which indicates balance and adaptability, the rigid hand portrays an inflexible, contracted individual with lots of pent-up energy. People with rigid hands need to 'move their energy out' in constructive ways (through sports, gardening, or other activity) in order to avoid stress-related diseases like hypertension, strokes, heart disease, ulcers, migraines and back pain.

THE LINES

In regard to health, the lines have a unique system of meaning within the structure of the hand. They indicate our degree of emotional balance and expression, our level of physical vitality, and our vulnerability to trauma, including illness, close calls with death and accidents.

Of all the lines of the hand, everyone is most concerned with the line of vitality or *life line*. The life line is the first to develop in embryonic life, and its depth, clarity and length reveal our level of vitality and physical constitution.

As pointed out earlier, the line of life moves down the hand towards the wrist from where the thumb meets the index finger. The top of the line shows the time of birth, while the bottom (where it begins to curve at the wrist) is at approximately seventy years of age. As the central line of the hand (everybody should have one), the life line records all major events including diseases, brushes with death, major life transitions, traumas, and loss of strength and vitality. The broken life line shown in Figure 9.1 indicates a life-threatening operation when the individual was in her mid-twenties. The young woman barely survived the operation

Figure 9.1: Hand print showing broken life line.

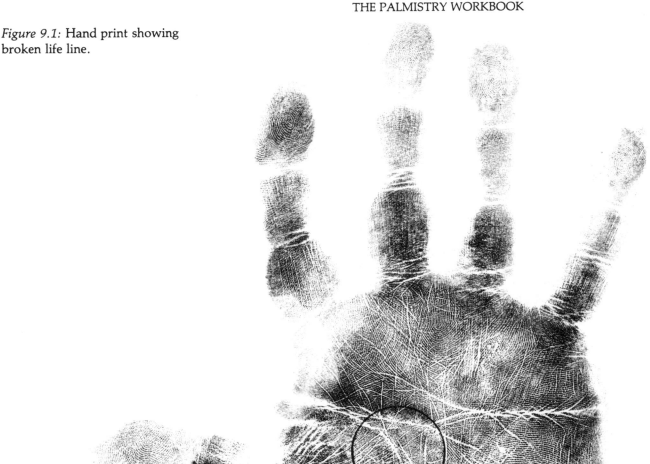

and her body temperature soared to 108 degrees as she left the operating room. The doctors had to pack her in ice for twenty-four hours, when her temperature began to subside. No one had expected her to recover. It is also interesting to note the small line of influence which moves through the break and touches the head line. The woman's close call with dying had a profound effect on her attitude towards life, and led to greater creativity and personal freedom.

However, since the life line can change, future life events and indications of illness are subject to change. All diseases, traumas and other difficulties — although often painful and sometimes life-threatening — have positive components. They teach us valuable lessons in vulnerability, dealing with frustration, taking responsibility for our health, and learning how to appreciate what we have in life.

Figure 9.2: **Hand print showing clear, broken life line.**

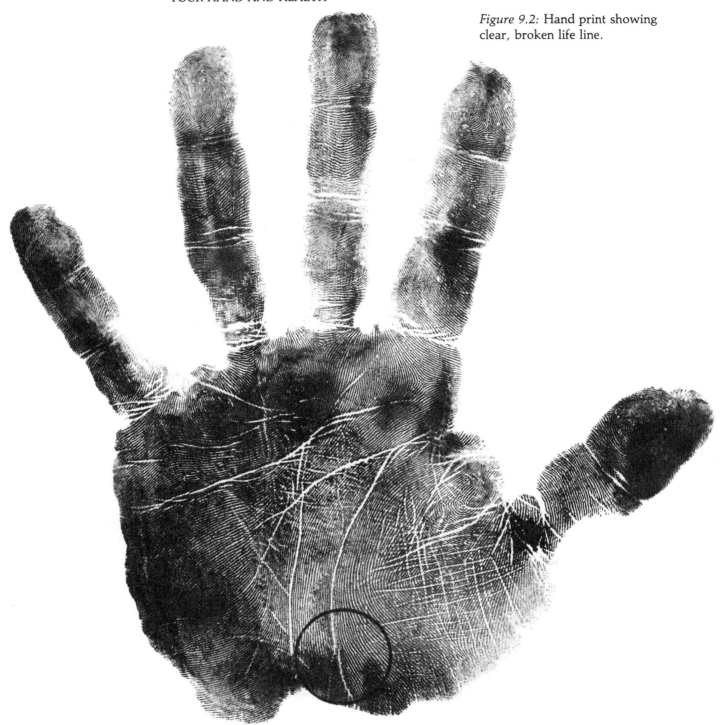

Can such problems be avoided? Perhaps. By becoming aware of — and working through — the lessons we need to learn during our lifetime *without* having to be jarred into action by an illness or other trauma, we may be able to avoid them later on. One case in point are the prints of a thirty-four-year-old lawyer, as shown in Figure 9.2. His life line was broken at approximately sixty-five years of age, which could indicate a life-threatening disease. Concerned about this possibility, he decided to improve his diet and cut down on smoking. Within several years, the

Figure 9.3: Hand print showing mended life line.

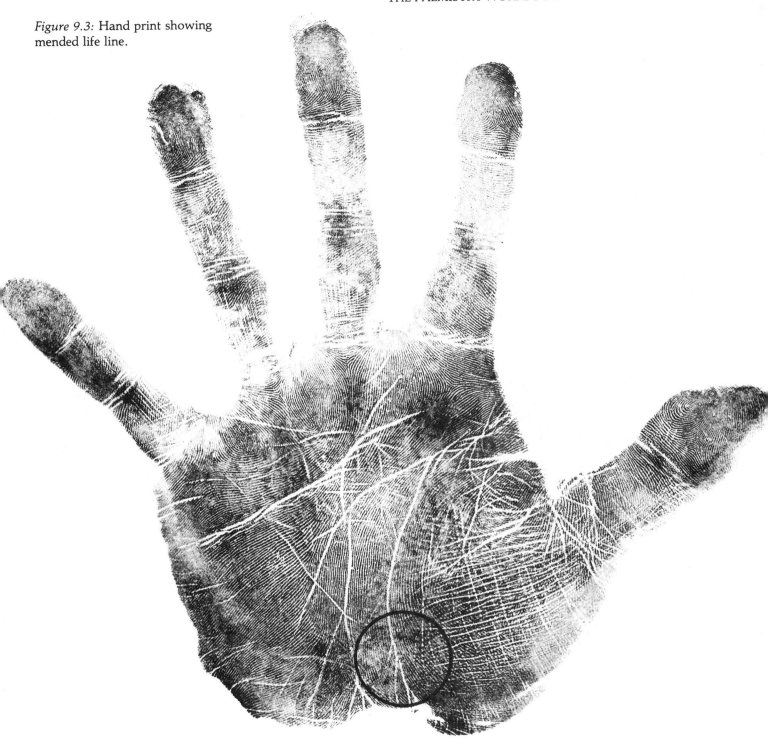

line mended completely (Figure 9.3). The possibility of a serious disease helped him adopt positive lifestyle habits. He took responsibility for his health *before* symptoms appeared.

A long, clear and deep life line (Figure 9.2) indicates vitality and a strong constitution, while a short or weak line full of islands and breaks (Figure 9.4) reveals physical weakness and increased vulnerability to disease. This type of life line does not necessarily condemn us to a short

100

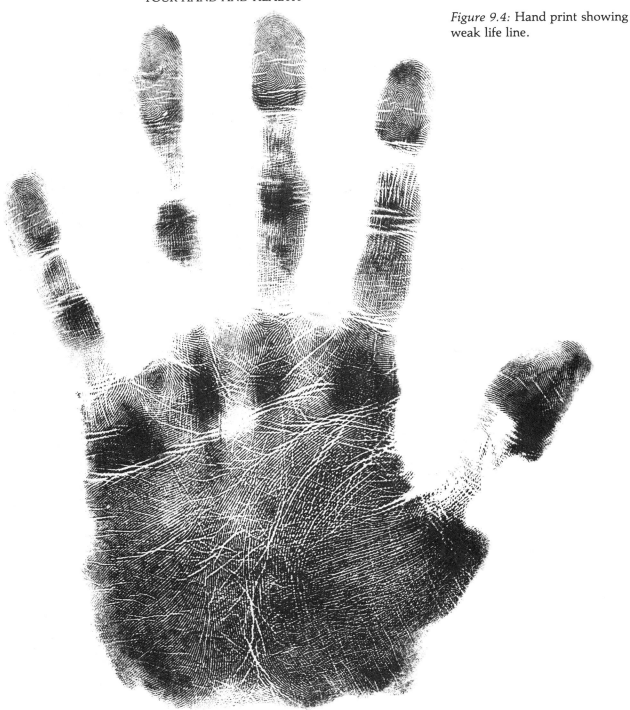

Figure 9.4: Hand print showing weak life line.

life or ill health. It indicates that we should never take our health for granted and be especially careful to eat properly, exercise regularly, and deal with minor health problems before they become major diseases. By making the conscious decision to adopt positive lifestyle habits, we can gradually change a weak, broken or short life line into one that is clear, long and strong.

Islands on the life line often indicate periods of low vitality and increased vulnerability to disease. If they happen to correspond in time with islands on the head, heart or career line, they can often take on a symbolic meaning to indicate confusion, worry, or lack of direction and focus. An egg-shaped island at the end of the life line is sometimes found on people with cancer. While this is no guarantee that one will suffer from cancer, it does indicate a predisposition to the disease. People with this island shouldn't panic, but need to eliminate the proven contributory factors which can lead to cancer: smoking, foods high in fat and additives but low in fibre, environmental pollution and chronic stress. They should also be aware of the 'seven cancer danger signals' and immediately bring them to the attention of a physician if any appear.

Figure 9.5: Hand print showing Saturn line performing as supplementary life line.

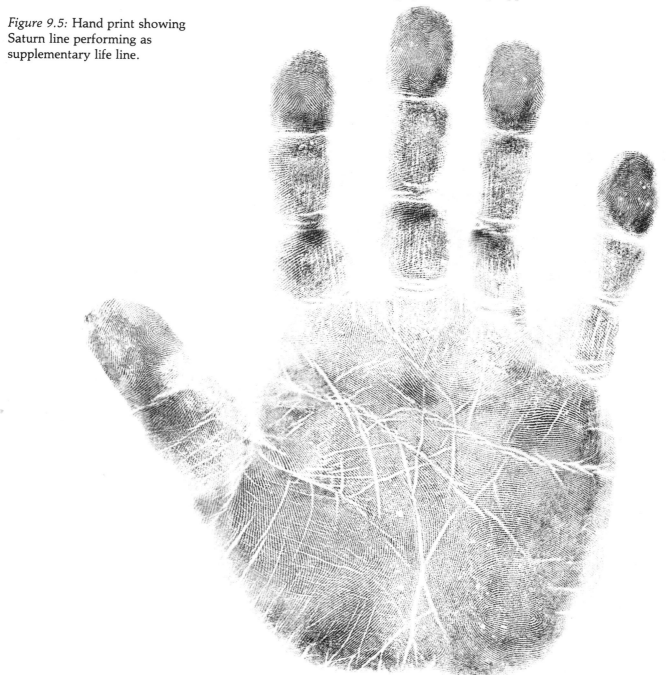

Red or blue dots appearing on the life line often indicate a serious illness or an accident involving a high fever. If a corresponding dot appears on the heart, head or stomach line at the same age, that organ will most likely be affected, especially if the dot appears on both hands.

If the life line is broken by an influence line coming from the mount of Venus, a serious accident may be indicated. Check both hands for verification.

The *inner life line* (Figure 9.1) runs parallel to the line of life, and provides added strength during illness, accident or loss of vitality. In this print, this short line 'covers' the break in the life line, and modifies its effect.

At times the Saturn line takes over the task of a weak or disappearing life line, as shown in Figure 9.5. In this case, the Saturn line performs 'double duty' and is both a supplementary life line and an indicator of career direction.

We mentioned earlier that a good *head line* is clear, strong, and free from islands and breaks. From a health perspective, islands indicate periods of worry or indecision which can lead to tension and stress-related diseases. If you have an island or break in your head line, you need to avoid mental stress and aggravation. Eat foods which relax rather than stimulate, avoid caffeine and refined sugars, and give yourself frequent periods of relaxation, recreation and meditation.

The *heart line* measures our emotional life and records many physical and emotional traumas. A broken or chained heart line reveals a high degree of emotional sensitivity which can in turn indicate a predisposition for stress-related diseases. Blue or red dots on the heart line are possible indicators of heart trouble or circulatory disease.

The *Mercury line* (or stomach line) begins near the end of the life line and moves upward towards the Mercury finger. Doctors tell us that it is better not to have this line at all, because its presence indicates possible trouble with the stomach, intestines, liver, pancreas and kidneys.

The abdomen and solar plexus have been called 'the mirror of the emotions'. When we repress feelings of anger, grief, and frustration, they can 'implode' and cause abdominal pain and dysfunction. While a strong and unbroken stomach line indicates a greater degree of resistance to abdominal problems, a broken line reveals present or potential ulcers, chronic intestinal cramps, colitis, or glandular problems due to emotional or other problems. The print shown in Figure 9.6 is that of a young man suffering from severe colitis. Specific problems, such as liver disease, are often recognized by a yellowish tinge to the nails or skin.

SKIN PATTERNS AND HEALTH

During the past few years, medical doctors and other scientists have discovered that ridge patterns or *dermoglyphics* on the palm and fingertips can be reliable indicators of certain physical and emotional conditions. The study of skin ridges — or *chiroglyphics* — is a fascinating science, but is still in its infancy. Some hand readers are beginning to rely on the study of dermoglyphics to evaluate emotional and physical health. However, with the following exceptions, most determinations based on skin ridges are rather speculative and should be taken with the proverbial grain of salt.

Figure 9.6: Hand print showing broken line of Mercury.

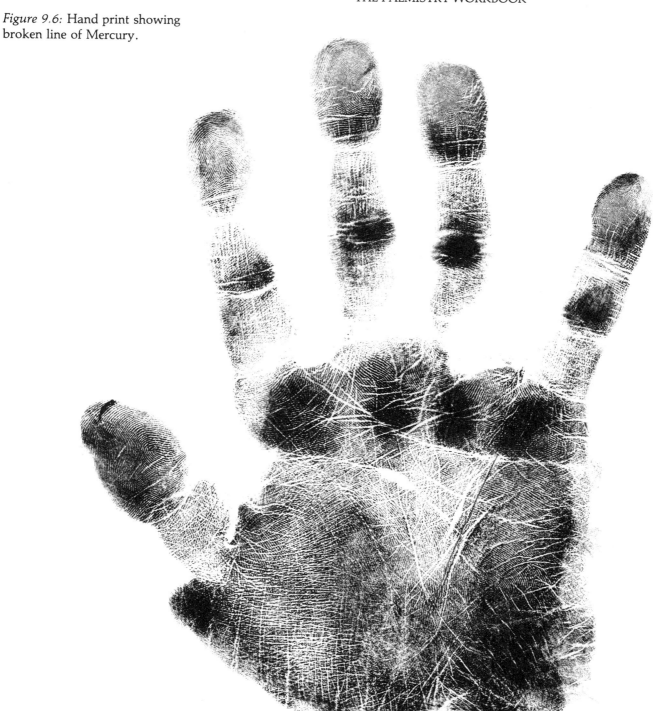

Our hands are patterned with various systems of parallel rows of dermoglyphics that are unique for each human being. Whenever these ridges meet, a *triradius* is formed. Four distinct triradii are found just under (and sometimes between) the fingers above the heart line, which we have already described as *apexes* of the various mounts. In addition,

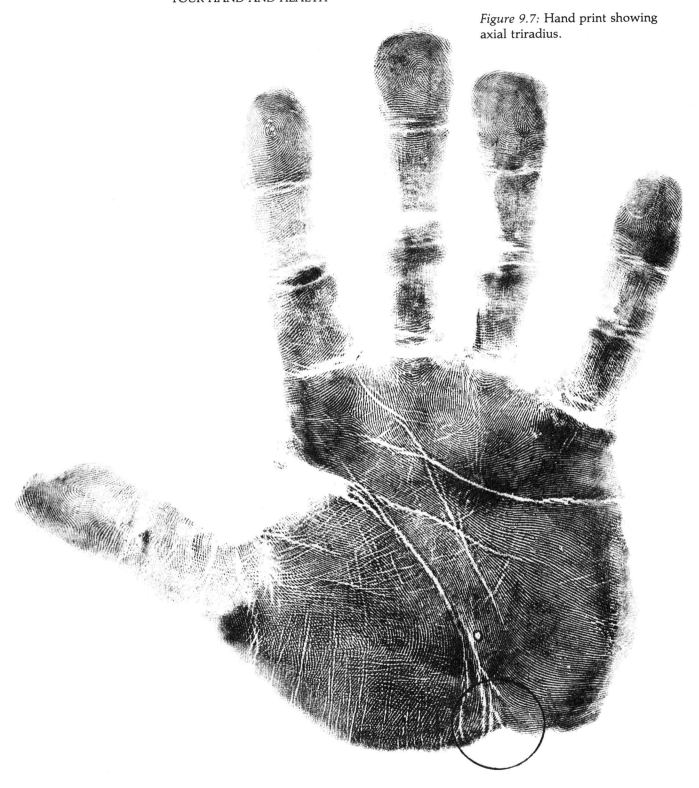

Figure 9.7: Hand print showing axial triradius.

there is one major triradius (known as the *axial triradius*) which is located at the base of the palm just above the wrist, as seen in Figure 9.7. According to the *Journal of the American Medical Association*, a displacement of

105

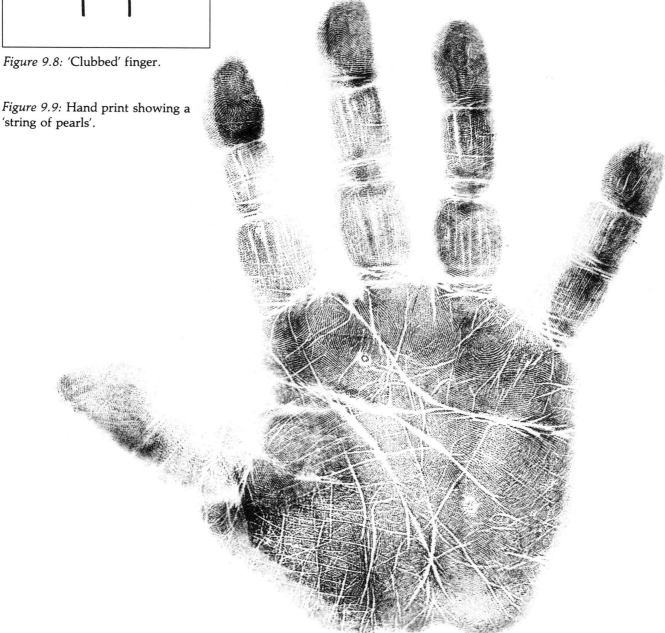

the axial triradius to a higher location on the palm can indicate a predisposition to congenital heart disease.

Another sign of heart disease exists when previously normal fingers tend towards 'clubbing' (Figure 9.8). Although clubbed fingers may be an inherited trait, their presence — especially with watchglass or Hippocratic nails, discussed later — indicate a tendency towards heart and lung disorders. When accompanied by a displaced axial triradius, present or potential heart disease is a good possibility.

When dermoglyphics are ill formed or disassociated, a 'string of pearls' (Figure 9.9) is present, and can reveal a predisposition to neurosis. Whorls or loops on the mount of Luna, an abnormal number of skin

Figure 9.8: 'Clubbed' finger.

Figure 9.9: Hand print showing a 'string of pearls'.

ridges, or a high frequency of whorls on the fingertips (Figure 9.10) can all indicate congenital heart defects. Consult *A Doctor's Guide to Better Health Through Palmistry* (see Bibliography) for a more complete discussion.

NAILS: THEIR UNPOLISHED MESSAGE

The nails are the first tissues of the body surface to develop, and sometimes appear as early as the ninth week of prenatal life. While the nails come in a wide variety of colours, shapes and sizes, the 'ideal' nail should be slightly longer than wide, more elastic than brittle, be gently curved, and healthy pink in colour.

In addition to revealing basic personality traits, medical doctors have used the nail as an aid to diagnose endocrine disturbances, circulatory problems, anaemia and other diseases. Although medical diagnosis through the nails is still a young science, careful examination of the nails can tell you many things about character and health and should be a part of every hand analysis. However, be sure to correlate your findings with other signs on the hand before making an evaluation.

Colour

Pink nails that are smooth and slightly lustrous reveal a balanced mental disposition, adequate nutritional intake, and good general health. *Red nails* indicate stronger blood circulation and a tendency for flashes of anger, over-excitement, and hypertension. People with red nails should avoid caffeine and other stimulants, and learn how to relieve pent-up emotions through exercise, creative activity (such as gardening, art, or carpentry) and regular meditation.

Blue or bluish nails indicate circulatory problems. If all the nails on both hands are bluish, the disturbance is more generalized, while several blue or bluish nails reveal a local circulatory problem. If the nails are bluish and the person has no circulatory complaints, chances are that their personality is somewhat reserved and cold. Warmth and passion are hidden behind a façade of cool equilibrium and restraint. Body work (such as Reichian therapy or bioenergetics), jogging, handball, fencing, the martial arts and other dynamic exercise techniques are often helpful in increasing blood circulation to the extremities and help us express our emotions more directly and fully.

Pale nails — like pale skin — indicate low vitality and poor nutrition, while *yellowish nails* may reveal liver trouble.

White dots or *spots* on the nails are general signs of anxiety or stress, and are often found on people who suffer from chronic depression. They may also indicate a calcium deficiency, especially if the nails are soft.

Moons should ideally appear on all the fingernails and indicate good health and a strong constitution. Their absence altogether may indicate an underactive thyroid gland (especially if the nails are brittle, ridged and short) while abnormally large moons (moons that fill over a third of the nail surface) indicate general weakness and an overactive thyroid gland.

Figure 9.10: A whorl finger print pattern.

Figure 9.11: Fan-shaped nail.

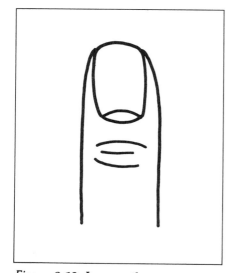

Figure 9.12: Long nail.

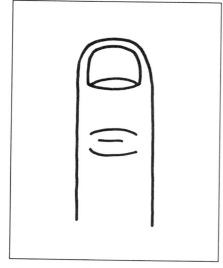

Figure 9.13: Short nail.

Shapes

Fingernails come in a variety of shapes, but for the purpose of health analysis, we will deal with five basic types: fan-shaped nails; long, narrow nails; short nails; watchglass or Hippocratic nails; and spoon nails.

Fan-shaped and *long, narrow nails* (Figures 9.11 and 9.12) reveal an individual prone to chronic nervousness with a low tolerance for frustration. These people often suffer from nervous disorders and psychosomatic diseases.

Short nails (Figure 9.13) are often found on people who are highly critical and impatient towards themselves, other people, and life in general. Heart trouble and depression have been linked to short nails.

Hippocratic or *'watchglass' nails* (Figure 9.14) are curved in the shape of a watch crystal. They indicate a general weakness of the respiratory system, and have been found on people who are heavy smokers, sufferers of tuberculosis and other lung diseases. Hippocratic nails can also reveal a predisposition for heart disease (especially if the nails are bluish in colour) and cirrhosis of the liver (especially if the nails are yellowish in colour). Whenever you see a person with watchglass nails (even when the curvature is mild) you should advise that he or she stop smoking if they do so, and to seek out as pollution-free an environment as possible.

Spoon nails (Figure 9.15) are concave in appearance, and reveal nutritional deficiencies (especially in iron), an underactive thyroid gland, and the possible presence of chronic skin disorders.

Lines, ridges and other signs

Healthy nails are well-proportioned in size, are strong without being brittle, are healthy pink in colour, and have between 75 and 100 fine parallel shallow ridges from the base of the nail moving vertically to the top.

Beau's lines (Figure 9.16) are deep horizontal ridges or 'dents' which begin at the root of the nail and move upwards as the nail grows. They are associated with nervous shock, acute infections, nutritional deficiencies, and other major physical and emotional traumas.

Mee's lines (Figure 9.17) are similar to Beau's lines, but do not form dents in the nail surface. They are considered to be indicators of high fever, arsenic poisoning, and coronary heart disease.

Unlike Beau's lines or Mee's lines, which reveal acute disorders, well-marked *longitudinal ridges* (Figure 9.18) are often associated with chronic diseases like colitis, long-standing skin disorders, rheumatism and hyperthyroidism.

Soft nails which split easily often indicate some kind of nutritional deficiency (especially in protein and calcium) and are often found on people suffering from arthritis. *Brittle* and *broken nails* can be a sign of an underactive thyroid or pituitary gland.

Although there is no foolproof method for diagnosing disease, a careful and thorough study of the human hand can provide a wealth of information regarding predisposition to a wide variety of health conditions and the actual presence of disease or deficiency. While there is no single method for diagnosing and evaluating our general state of health, medical palmistry can be of tremendous value — either alone or in conjunction with other diagnostic techniques — to make us aware of what prevents us from enjoying optimum health. Since it is *the body which heals itself,* hand analysis can guide us towards taking personal responsibility for our health and adopt lifestyle habits that will enable us to enjoy healthy, active and productive lives.

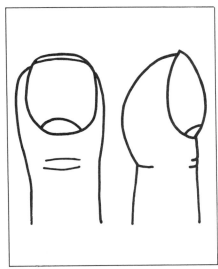

Figure 9.14: Hippocratic or 'watchglass' nail.

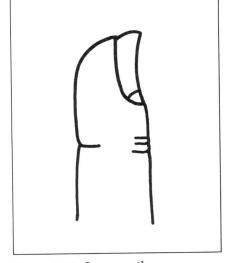

Figure 9.15: Spoon nail.

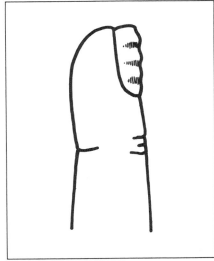

Figure 9.16: Beau's lines.

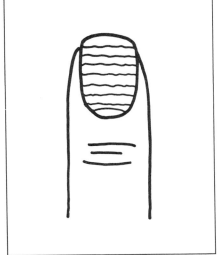

Figure 9.17: Mee's lines.

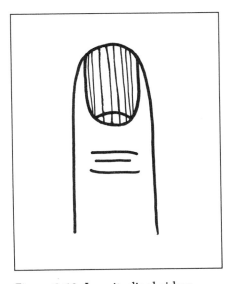

Figure 9.18: Longitudinal ridges.

Chapter 10

YOUR HAND AND THE SPIRITUAL LIFE

Throughout human history, sages have taught that we possess a spiritual centre or *core.* As the principle of conscious life which animates our being, it has been referred to as the Christ Within, the higher self and the *Atman.* Dr John C. Pierrakos, co-founder of the Institute for the New Age wrote:

> Core consciousness is universal consciousness. Our core is the well spring of awareness, our font of communion with outer reality, our nucleus for self-expression . . . Moving from the core, from the higher self, means moving towards fulfilment of our greatest potential.

The goal of spiritual evolution is to become conscious of this inner core and help it manifest in our lives.

When considering the human hand from a spiritual point of view, we need to bear in mind that living a spiritual life does not necessarily involve escaping from the world, nor does it call for the repression of our lower nature. Rather, it is grounded in the conscious awareness of *what is* and the integration of our physical body, thoughts and emotions with our spiritual centre or *core.* Unlike the old religious images of asceticism and denial, the goal of spirituality is essentially the establishment of right human relations, the promotion of goodwill, and doing our part — whatever it is — towards establishing peace on Earth. In addition to this outer work, spirituality also implies deepening our connection with our higher self and with the universal consciousness some people call God.

Over the years, serious hand readers have been concerned with the ability of hand analysis to help guide us towards developing our spiritual potential. Unfortunately, however, several myths still persist regarding what constitutes a 'spiritual' hand. In most books, long, tapered fingers are seen as a good indication of spiritual potential, along with the presence of mystic crosses, lines of intuition, Seals of Solomon and other signs. In some cases the existence of these markings in the hand has become a status symbol among students of occultism ('Hey, take a look at my Mystic Cross!'). There has also been a tendency among chirologists to stress the importance of developing psychic ability over developing one's intuition and spiritual consciousness through meditation and selfless service.

In the following pages we will explore how a deep understanding of the human hand can help us — and those we counsel — to achieve our spiritual potential. Because the hand is the mirror of our spiritual essence as expressed through our personality, talents and mental ability, we will see how — by studying basic hand types and markings — we can expand our awareness, develop the intuition, and come into deeper contact with our spiritual core. By integrating these aspects into daily life, we can discover new avenues of spiritual unfoldment and service according to our energies, talents and aspirations.

All types of hands — be they square, spatulate or psychic — express essential qualities' which enable us to reach spiritual fulfilment and the expansion of consciousness. While these qualities are important by themselves, the hand may also indicate what is needed to achieve a deeper level of personal integration and balance in life. In many cases, especially when there is dissatisfaction and frustration, the existence of a particular quality may indicate the need to develop a *complementary* quality in order to fully integrate the personality. For example, those who are primarily intellectual might strive to develop the emotional nature, while the person who is primarily sensate, might need to develop the intuition.

While the following brief descriptions of hand types are valuable in evaluating spiritual potential and expression, special attention should be given to the important modifying factors such as lines, mounts, finger spacing, skin texture and flexibility.

SPATULATE HANDS

The classic spatulate hand can be classified as sensate. Keywords used to describe spatulate hands include action, innovation, and the ability to get things done. Well-grounded in three-dimensional reality, people with spatulate hands are basically sensuous, impulsive and practical. They are not afraid of new ideas, nor are they afraid of moving forward into unfamiliar areas of activity and study. These characteristics are often found in leaders of religious groups and organizers of spiritual events, as well as fundraisers and evangelists. In spiritual matters — as with all areas of life — there is an enthusiasm to discover, learn, overcome obstacles and move ahead.

When there are knots in the fingers, the capacity for analyzing is increased, which — along with joined head and heart lines — will reduce an innate impulsiveness while increasing introspection, a quality often lacking in people with spatulate hands. Receptivity may also need to be developed, along with the ability to sit quietly and 'go inside'. If the first phalange of the thumb is thin, there may be a need to reduce stress through exercise, diet and meditation. The goal would be to increase receptivity while acknowledging the active and dynamic qualities which spatulate hands represent.

SQUARE HANDS

The square hand reflects primarily an intellectual character. Common sense, order, method and determination are several of the essential qualities the squarish hand represents. Administrators, researchers and teachers often reflect the capacities shown in square hands, as do those who are often drawn to traditional religious teachings. They love order, rules and stability, and can express their ideas in a well organized manner. While the spatulate hand may express the spiritual principle of 'spirituality in action', the square hand might reflect the principle of 'divine order and authority'.

However, there is often a tendency to be afraid of change and be closed to new ideas, especially if the hand is rigid. While healthy scepticism is often useful, people with square fingertips (especially if the fingernails are naturally short) are often critical and demand that an idea be proven beyond any shadow of a doubt before they will accept it. In cases where the hand and thumb are stiff, the ability to share — be they feelings, ideas or possessions — is an important spiritual lesson to learn in life.

Another major goal involves the development of the sensate and emotional aspects of the personality. People with square hands need to be more spontaneous and learn how to 'let go'. While the owner of the spatulate hand may need to take up meditation and organize his or her life, the square-handed individual might consider devoting themself to yoga (to develop flexibility), active sports (to mobilize physical energy) and aerobic dancing and ballet to help 'get out of the head' and become more in tune with body rhythms.

CONIC HANDS

Those with conic or artistic hands have little trouble being in touch with their feelings. They are governed by their emotions and are often drawn to things spiritual. Pointed fingers in general reveal a keen appreciation of nature, while a pointed Jupiter finger in particular (especially if it is long and is accompanied by a strong mount) reflects a strong inspirational and devotional current. Meditation, prayer, chanting and drugs are often used by those with conic fingers to achieve their spiritual ideal. They are often drawn to psychism, especially if there is a pronounced mount of Luna with strong lines of intuition. Their capacity to express spiritual ideals through beauty and art is especially notable, as is their innate ability to support others in their spiritual endeavours.

However, people with conic hands (especially if the thumb and hand itself are flexible) have difficulty being consistent, and have a tendency to move quickly from one spiritual group or teaching to another without developing a sense of depth or commitment. They can also be capricious, and are easily swayed by moods. If the hands are thick and soft, there can be an inordinate love for material things and the tendency to focus on sensate aspects of life.

Generally speaking, the owners of conic hands need to develop the intellect. They need to analyse and question more, and not be swayed by sentiment and impulse. When the fingers are smooth, there is a need to focus more on details. The development of order, tact, responsibility and consistency are also major keys to their spiritual integration.

In cases where the hands are thin and crossed by many lines, it may be appropriate to suggest a diet containing whole grains and pulses, with a minimum of processed sugar, red meat, harsh spices and other stimulants in order to reduce nervous tension and help stabilize the emotions. Yoga and meditation are good complements to such a diet. Finally, spirituality through *service* on a practical level is an important spiritual path for those with conic hands.

PSYCHIC HANDS

Although psychic hands are extremely rare in their pure form, they reveal a natural affinity for spirituality and religion. This type of hand reflects all the positive aspects of the conic hand, where love of beauty, harmony and religious inspiration are pronounced. Meditation, prayer and philosophy (especially when the fingers are knotted) are favoured with this type of hand.

However, there is a need to be more grounded in the 'nuts and bolts' of daily living (or at least to have someone else occupy themselves with such details). Because people with psychic hands are highly sensitive, they require pure food and a minimum of alcohol, tobacco, sugar and other toxins. Drug abuse can also be a problem for those with psychic hands. Because there is a tendency to get lost in dreams and be apart from day-to-day reality, contact with the Earth — through activities such as gardening and taking long walks in the country — are useful. Exercise is also important, especially those forms which strengthen the legs and ankles. The need for strong and stable friendships is essential for these people, especially with friends who provide a 'grounding' influence.

'PHILOSOPHICAL' HANDS

Hands with knotty joints form a special classification for this chapter, and characterize the religious thinker and scholar. Like the owner of the square hand type, those with knotty fingers are logical, reasonable and studious. Such hands are often found in India among yogis, ascetics and philosophers.

When viewed in a spiritual context, people with these hands are not seduced by appearances, and have the ability to penetrate deeply into the nature of truth and reality. Being inherently patient, they are careful and thorough in their undertakings. As teachers and writers, they can examine all sides of a question and analyze concepts often passed over by others.

However, such individuals can often get lost in detail and not perceive the totality of an issue, especially if their fingers are both knotted and long. There may also be a tendency to lose oneself in idealistic concepts without being grounded in everyday reality. A classic example would be a scholar well versed in Hermetic philosophy, but who forgets to eat his dinner and has a habit of losing his keys.

In some cases, the analytical understanding of spiritual matters is developed at the expense of intuitional perception. As part of the process of spiritual integration, qualities like playfulness, emotionality and body awareness should be developed as much as possible.

MIXED HANDS

The mixed hand is by far the most common you will see, and by definition reflects many of the traits discussed in the preceding pages. These hands will reveal a complexity of currents, talents and abilities, including an ease to adapt to new circumstances and an openness to unfamiliar teachings and spiritual practices. While such hands reveal a strong mystical tendency (especially if the Jupiter finger is long and tapered and a mystic cross or Seal of Solomon is in evidence) there is an ability to express spiritual understanding in practical terms.

When analyzing the mixed hand in a spiritual context, try to be aware of the hand type or types which seem to predominate. Is the hand basically square, conic or spatulate? Which finger or fingers are the strongest? What are the outstanding mounts? What do the lines reveal? Is the hand more receptive, or is the energy more assertive? Is the hand fleshy or thin? Is it rigid or does it bend? By developing an analytical technique based on sensitivity and careful attention to detail, we can gradually achieve a feel for the person's spiritual being and offer insights which can help him or her connect with their spiritual needs and move forward with their life task.

THE LINES

Particular lines of the hand can offer additional insights into spiritual direction and unfoldment.

The *heart line*, as mentioned before, indicates the depth and quality of the emotions. In a spiritual context, these emotions — when properly channelled — are essential in helping us attain our spiritual goals.

Generally speaking, a long, deep or otherwise predominating heart line reveals a person who is oriented towards universal brotherhood and service to humanity. Contact with other people is favoured, whether as a spiritual teacher, healer or administrator. Shorter or more 'physical' heart lines can indicate devotion on a more personal scale, such as towards a particular religious figure or group. The large fleshy hand and strong physical heart line of John B. S. Coats, late International President of The Theosophical Society (Figure 10.1) reflect a balance of these attributes. Though known as an inspiring teacher and articulate lecturer, he is primarily remembered for his warm, sympathetic heart and wonderful sense of humour. While committed to a universal ideal, he was known to thousands of people around the world, most of whom considered him a special personal friend.

The *head line* is a good indicator of spiritual direction. When the head line predominates over the heart line, the individual will be drawn more towards study, writing and meditation than devotion and

Figure 10.1: Hand print showing strong physical heart line.

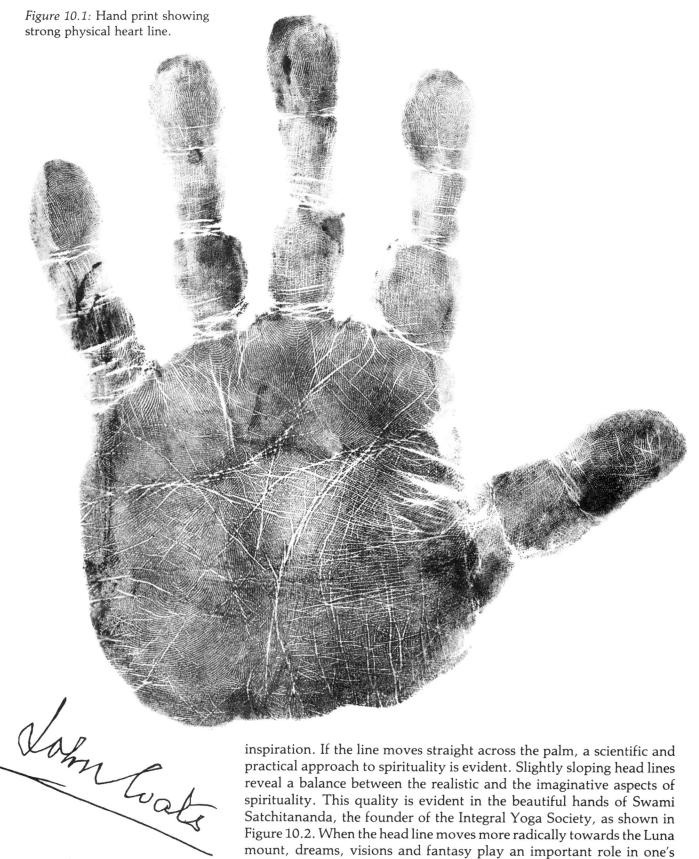

inspiration. If the line moves straight across the palm, a scientific and practical approach to spirituality is evident. Slightly sloping head lines reveal a balance between the realistic and the imaginative aspects of spirituality. This quality is evident in the beautiful hands of Swami Satchitananda, the founder of the Integral Yoga Society, as shown in Figure 10.2. When the head line moves more radically towards the Luna mount, dreams, visions and fantasy play an important role in one's

Figure 10.2: The hands of Swami Satchitananda.

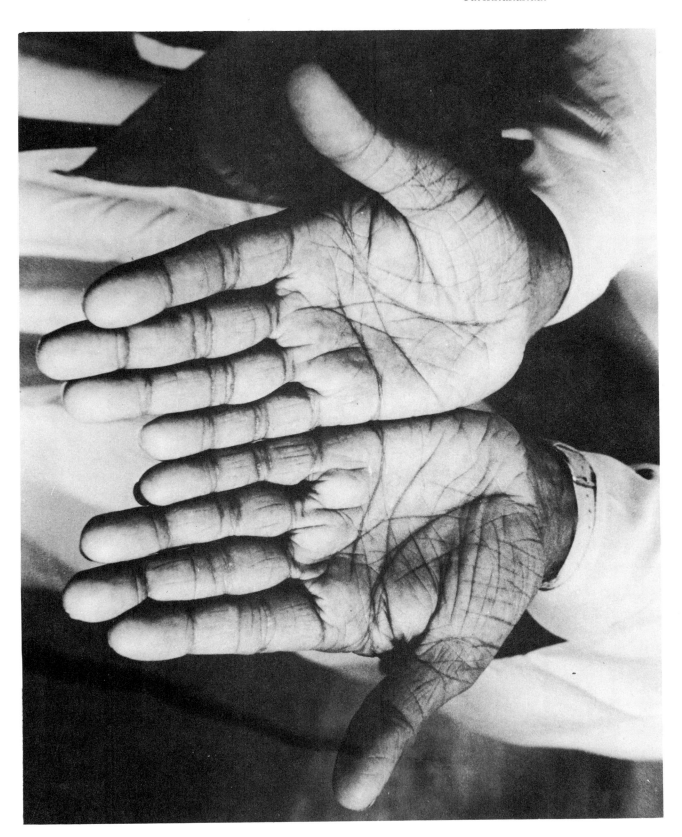

spiritual life. The positive aspects of such a line include an ability to easily grasp abstract or esoteric subjects, while the negative aspects include a tendency to 'space out' and not be able to translate spiritual understanding into daily practice. As pointed out earlier, islands on the head line indicate worry or lack of mental concentration. In such cases, meditation can help relieve anxiety and focus the mind.

Lines of intuition begin in the mount of Luna and move towards the centre of the palm. They indicate strong intuitive ability and the tendency to follow one's instincts rather than rely on analysis. When a single line of intuition moves from the mount of Luna and forms a gentle arc towards the mount of Mercury, strong psychic ability may be present. This line, known as the *line of Uranus*, is often found on the hands of

Figure 10.3: Hand print showing the line of Uranus.

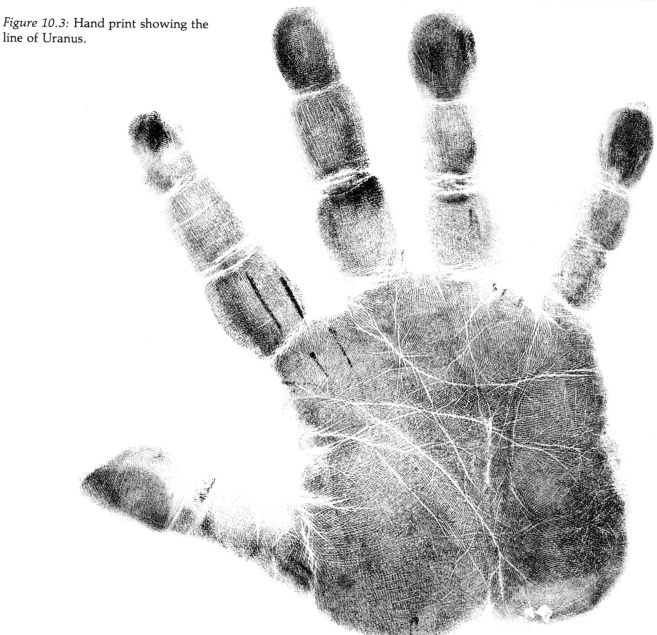

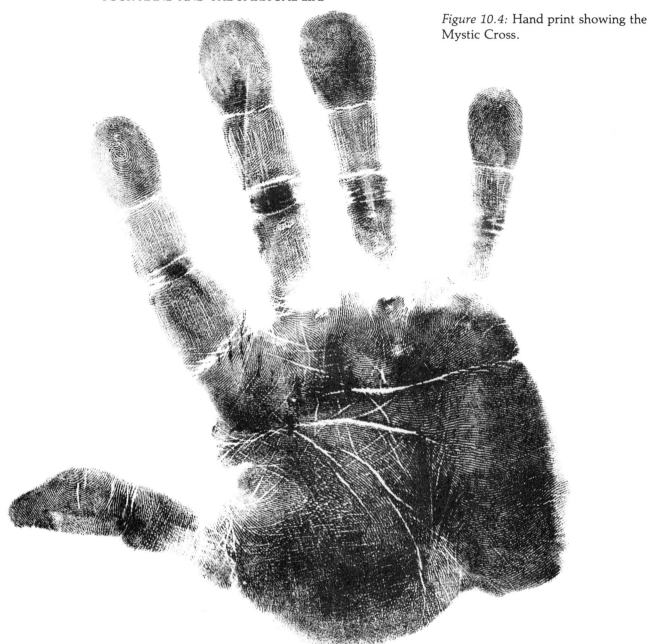

Figure 10.4: Hand print showing the Mystic Cross.

mediums and clairvoyants, such as on that of Gloria B., a gifted clairvoyant and healer (Figure 10.3).

The *Seal of Solomon* is also found on Gloria's hand. It consists of a diagonal line (often in the form of an arc) which passes through the mount of Jupiter. This marking shows a strong interest in metaphysics, occultism, and unorthodox religion. People with this line, which is found on perhaps five per cent of the population, are often drawn to mysticism, yoga, astrology and other New Age teachings.

The *Mystic Cross* is considered a sign of strong interest in spiritual development. Appearing as a cross between the lines of heart and head, it is not the result of two long lines (such as the Saturn line and an influence line from Venus) but rather is formed by two short lines which cross each

119

other, as seen in Figure 10.4. The hand is that of a young man who has been deeply involved with The Theosophical Society since early childhood.

It should be noted that the absence of these markings does not indicate any lack of spiritual development or capacity, nor should their existence be interpreted as a sign of special spiritual advancement. Rather, these signs — alone or collectively — are merely signposts which indicate certain interests and abilities.

Hand analysis provides a master key to help us understand our place in the universe. It teaches that each individual temperament is an equal and valid reflection of spiritual reality and shows how it can be expressed in a positive and dynamic way from our core. Above all, hand analysis can help us expand our inner vision while enabling us to release our positive unconscious forces to help others find creativity, pleasure and inner peace.

Chapter 11

CAREER AND SELF-FULFILMENT

Although good health and a satisfying relationship are major keys to happiness, surveys have shown that a fulfilling career is one of our most important personal concerns. Yet despite its importance, most people are frustrated with their work and often function in job situations which are boring, over-stressful, or offer few opportunities for advancement. While some people decide to 'tough it out' at an unfulfilling job with an eye towards retirement, others tend to move from job to job with little focus or commitment.

Ideally, our career should be more than just a job, or an activity which only contributes to our basic survival needs. It should also be a *vocation*, or an activity which provides a sense of self-fulfilment, self-worth, or contribution to society. While it need not occupy all of our talent, time and energy, a career should be conducive to our personal, professional and spiritual well-being. It should provide pleasure, challenge and opportunities for personal growth.

There are several factors which lead us to a career choice that are of interest to a hand reader. Perhaps the major influence comes from our parents. Whether the influence is conscious or not, our parents' desire to see us in a certain professional field is viewed as a major factor in career choice. Very often these 'secret contracts' we make with our parents lead us into professions for which we are totally unsuited.

In some cases, career choice involves a rebellion against parental pressure. Very often we abandon early areas of aptitude and interest to spite our parents, areas which might have offered the seeds for a fulfilling career. Sometimes we rediscover these childhood interests and skills. For this reason, career counsellors suggest that we become aware of the unconscious decisions we made years ago so that we can again respond to our primary interests and emotions.

There are other barriers to a fulfilling career. Like the early 'parental tapes' which continue to influence us during adulthood, we often harbour feelings of worthlessness and lack of self-esteem (usually shown by a short Jupiter finger and the joining of the lines of life and head). All too often the rest of the hand reveals an abundance of talent, skills and interests, while a poor self-image undermines the ability to manifest them in the world. While all of us need to take account of our limitations and imperfections, we also must release the old feelings of worthlessness and inadequacy we often carry with us from childhood.

It is also important to place work in its proper perspective. For many people, their job tends to compensate for a poor social life, or can be used as an escape from a difficult relationship or other problem. When work is used as an avoidance of other responsibilities or as a way to compensate for feelings of loneliness or despair, it will not create a feeling of well-being and satisfaction in the long run. Again, this trend can be noted in the hand, especially by examining the heart and union lines.

Age also has much to do with our professional reality. Every seven to ten years we go through important life cycles which reflect different personal and professional needs. While they very according to each individual, some basic life cycles are as follows:

Early years (20-30) A time for opportunities and exploration.
Building years (30-40) A time for solidifying our career choice. A period of dynamic changes in the form of traumas, problems and challenges.
Transitional years (40-50) A period of reduced economic pressure, with new opportunities for enjoyment and an increased desire for personal growth.
Mature years (50-60) Often seen as years of lowered enthusiasm and decline, this period may also be a time for new discoveries and professional direction.
Golden years (60+) Usually considered as a period of relaxation, loneliness or boredom, it can also be a time for utilizing our life experience and accumulated wisdom in new areas of creativity, pleasure and service.

These cycles show that life involves continuous changes. We need to manage these changes and adapt to our present needs.

Like other areas of importance, the hand is a 'living blueprint' of our professional life. While the shape and consistency of the hand, the texture of the skin, and the form and strength of the fingers offer information about our basic skills and career direction, the lines of the hand — and the Saturn line in particular — reveal the degree to which we are 'grounded' in a satisfying career path and the extent to which we are fulfilling our life task.

Because the lines can always change, the hand can offer us continuing guidance regarding career direction and personal fulfilment. It is important to remember that outer 'luck' does not create a vocation. However, by getting in touch with our deepest aspirations, talents and skills, we can begin to attract people, opportunities and circumstances which open the door to satisfying and purposeful careers.

The basic hand types reflect certain 'core qualities' which enable us to achieve fulfilment in life. At the same time, a basic quality may also point towards a need to develop a complementary or 'shadow' quality in order to obtain a greater level of personal integration and satisfaction. This is especially true when our career path appears stale or chronically frustrating. For example, for an accountant whose square hands and knotty fingers indicate organizing ability and an interest in detail and analysis, a possible career alternative may include working more with the theatre, the arts, or in an area where complementary qualities like intuition, spontaneity or emotion can be more integrated into the individual's work life. This may not necessarily involve a complete career change (i.e., from accountant to movie star), but rather a career *modification* which can include serving as a financial manager or consultant for a dance company, or taking up painting or acting purely as an avocation. Again, the point to remember is: If the person is happy with life, there is no problem. But if there is an overriding sense of restlessness or frustration, the 'other side' of the personality may need to be developed.

There is no rigid standard for success in one's career. While the 'passive' hand reveals our talents and possibilities, our dominant hand indicates the degree to which we are utilizing these capacities at the moment.

FIRST, THE MODIFIERS

Before we explore specific hand types, mounts and major lines in reference to career choice, let us first note several important modifying factors.

To the degree that the thumb is set high, low or medium, we can determine the level of self-confidence and independence. It will also indicate whether or not the temperament is introverted or extroverted.

The size and shape of the thumb can show the degree of ego strength, leadership and will power and how they relate to career choice and performance on the job.

If the head and life lines separate, the individual is impulsive, impatient, and self-reliant. The farther the lines are apart, the greater the self-confidence and extroversion.

When the head and life lines run together, the individual tends to be introverted, careful, and may lack self-confidence and self-esteem. The longer these lines connect, the more cautious and introverted the personality.

The greater the flexibility of the hand, the more adaptable and flexible the personality. People with extremely flexible hands tend to lack emotional stability, especially if confirming factors are present.

Finely textured skin reflects a sensitive nature, while coarse skin is found on people who are more 'rough and tumble'. A man with a strong, square hand with fine skin may be drawn to a white collar job like business administration, while his counterpart with coarsely textured skin wouldn't mind being a foreman on a construction site or manage a business selling spare parts.

HAND TYPES AND CAREER CHOICE

Square hands are useful hands. They reveal an ability to organize, persevere, and get things done. Order, stability and common sense are among the major qualities of the square hand, which make for precision, thoroughness and a systematic approach in dealing with ideas and projects.

Although skin texture, predominant fingers and lines can modify the qualities of squarish hands, it is often found in executives, organizers and politicians. Square hands are also common among administrative assistants, clerks and secretaries who have an ability to organize an office or business. Computer programmers and operators (especially if the fingers are knotted) are favoured by squarish hands, as are teachers (especially those who specialize in geometry and languages), engineers, lawyers, doctors, librarians and accountants. Landscape architecture and interior design are possible career choices as well, especially if the head line reveals a good imagination.

Spatulate hands are hands of action. They reveal a capacity to take advantage of a situation and use it in a practical way.

Like those with squarish hands, people with spatulate hands make good executives, although their strength is geared more towards leadership than administration. They make excellent entrepreneurs, businesspeople, managers and inventors. When healing ability is present (small vertical lines or *Samaritan lines* located on the mount of Mercury are a major indication of healing power) there is a special talent to heal through inspiration. Careers in massage therapy, counselling, teaching and dance therapy are favoured. Spatulate hands are also found on athletes, singers and dancers. When communication is favoured on the hand, public relations, advertising and design are good career choices.

When spatulate hands feature knotted fingers, a career involving analytical and diplomatic skills is indicated. When the thumb is strong as well, there is an innate ability to follow through an important idea or project.

Conic hands are creative hands. They reflect a love of beauty and an ability to beautify one's surroundings. Governed by inspiration rather than reason, people with conic hands are often idealistic and imaginative in their work environment.

In addition to any career in the arts — including theatre, dance, music and crafts — people with conic hands often excel in the fields of interior design, architecture, textile design, advertising and writing. When the consistency of the hands is thick, one recalls the hands of the professional chef whose efforts are largely devoted to sensuous, artistic, and often highly calorific creations.

Though it is possible that our hands will reflect one or more of the hand types just described, chances are that they will reveal a *combination* of attributes. In that case, it is especially important to pay special attention to each finger and evaluate how its qualities can influence career choice. If the Apollo finger is spatulate, for example, it can indicate a talent for public speaking, teaching or acting. If the Jupiter finger is square, it reveals strong administrative ability. By taking account of these two traits alone, a possible career in public relations, politics or business would be indicated.

THE MOUNTS

We also need to take account of the dominant mounts in evaluating career possibilities. Although mounts should be considered in a context of the hand as a whole, they can nonetheless provide valuable information regarding career direction and choice.

Jupiter

A strong Jupiter mount indicates leadership. While politics, religious leadership and business administration are viewed as standard career directions, people with a prominent Jupiter mount often find satisfaction in running a business, school or other organization, and are drawn to counselling, teaching and working with nature and animals. In general, however, people with strong Jupiter mounts prefer to be in a position of authority and independence on the job and often have difficulty working for others.

Saturn

Saturn is considered the mount of balance, and reflects such qualities as wisdom, soberness and responsibility. Unlike the Jupitarian, who is more social and outgoing, the pure Saturnine type prefers to work alone. For people with coarsely textured hands, work in agriculture, construction and environmental protection are good career choices. For others, mathematics (both teaching and research), engineering, physics, environmental science, and computer technology are possible areas of interest. A strong Saturn mount also favours philosophical and religious studies, writing (especially on scientific themes), clerical work, library science, antique or building restoration, research of all kinds, and detailed work in arts, crafts and design, especially if the fingers are knotted.

Apollo

A strong mount of Apollo is a sign of artistic flair, brilliance, and work with the public. Careers in applied and fine arts (including architecture, design, painting, sculpture, landscaping and graphic arts), the performing arts, advertising, public relations, sales and writing are favoured by a strong Apollo mount and finger. If this configuration is enhanced by a strong Mercury finger, the ability to communicate is strengthened, as shown by the hand of one of America's most distinguished character actors (Figure 11.1).

Other career possibilities for an Apollonian include teaching (especially when lecturing is involved), art and music therapy, and any job involving public contact such as receptionist, secretary, beautician, social worker or psychotherapist.

Mercury

Mercury is the mount of business and communication. People with a prominent mount of Mercury are known for their shrewdness, industry, and their ability to relate well to others. Careers in business, sales, banking and related fields are favoured by a strong mount and finger, while law, broadcasting, teaching, the natural sciences, transportation and language arts are other possible career directions. When Samaritan lines are present — as in the hand of the registered nurse shown in Figure 11.2 — a career in the health care field (including medicine, laboratory technology, psychology, osteopathy, chiropractic, dentistry or spiritual healing) is favoured.

Figure 11.1: Hand print showing a strong Apollo mount with a strong Mercury finger.

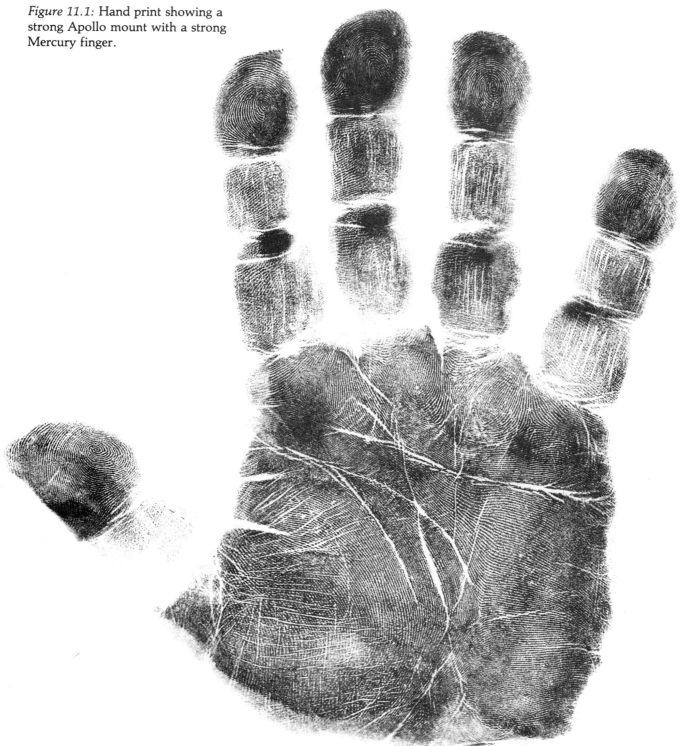

Mars

A strong mount of Mars reveals courage and resistance, with an ability to remain calm in the face of danger. Traditionally, hand readers have advised that people with strong mounts of Mars join the military services or police force, or take up professional boxing or wrestling as a career. Although these stereotyped ideas may have some validity (people with

126

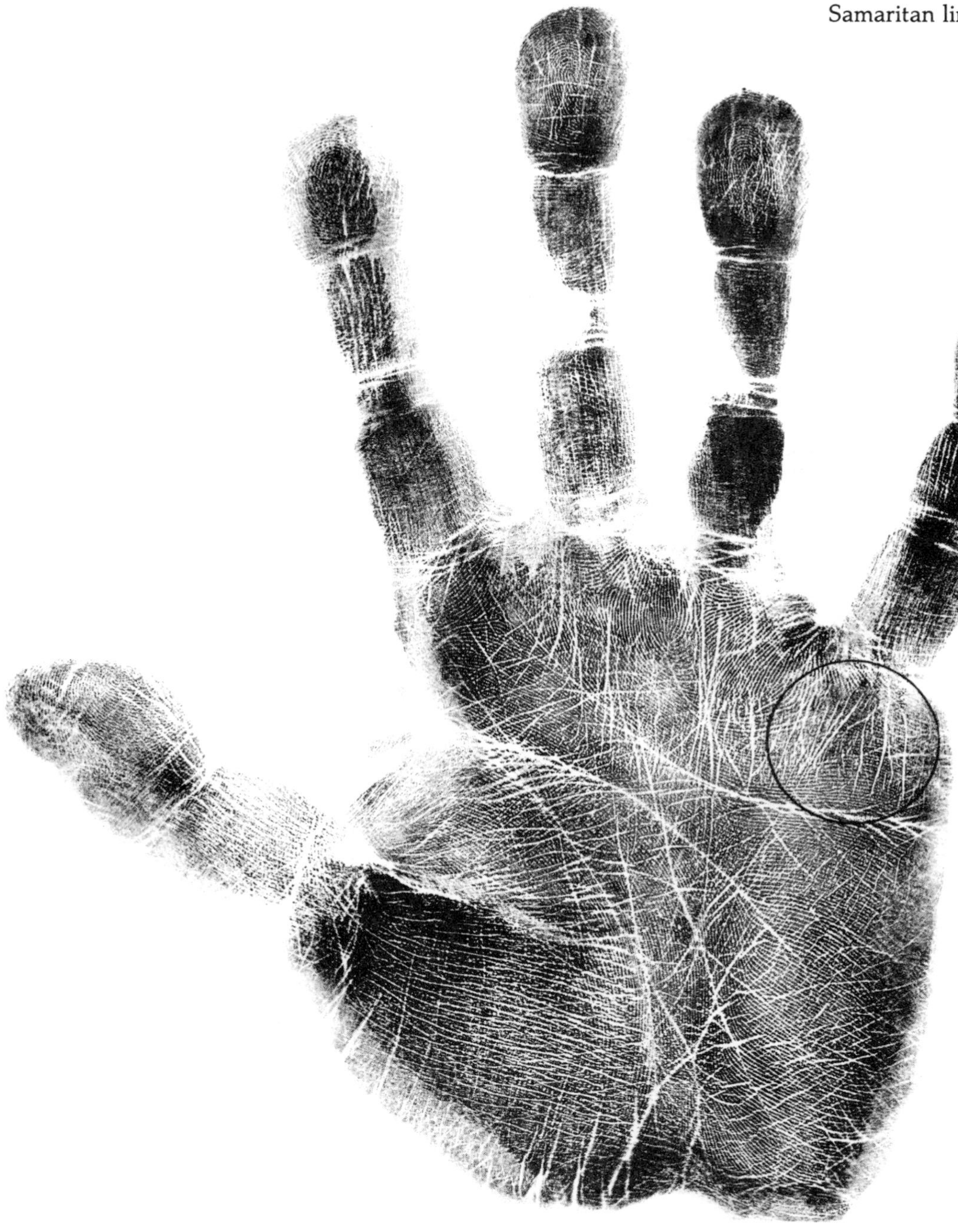

Figure 11.2: Hand print showing Samaritan lines.

strong Mars mounts *are* often drawn to military service and law enforcement) other career possibilities should be considered as well.

Men and women with strong mounts of Mars have a talent to work with three-dimensional reality. They love challenge and revel in accomplishment. Careers involving athletics and physical fitness, the building trades (including carpentry, masonry and plumbing), mechanics (involving automobiles, business machines or household appliances), manual labour, agriculture and environmental protection are possible areas of career interest.

Figure 11.3: Hand print showing small lines moving up from the base of Luna.

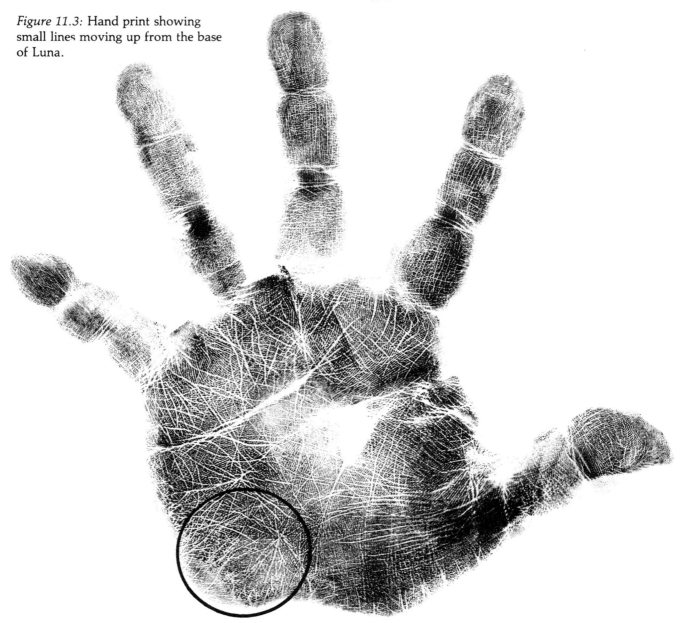

Luna

The lunar mount symbolizes imagination, love of travel, and our protective instincts toward friends and family. When the mount of Luna is well-developed (especially when accompanied by Samaritan lines on the mount of Mercury) a career in the 'helping professions', (like counselling, health care, social work or teaching) is indicated. Since the lunar mount also indicates a love of travel, any profession which involves movement is indicated. Pilots, flight attendants, professional drivers, travel agents and tour co-ordinators often possess strong mounts of Luna. A prominent lunar mount also enhances the imagination, and is frequently seen on the hands of accomplished writers, artists and composers. When small lines move upwards from the base of Luna, intuition and psychic ability are increased, as seen in the hand of a woman whose powerful intuition is applied to her counselling work (Figure 11.3).

128

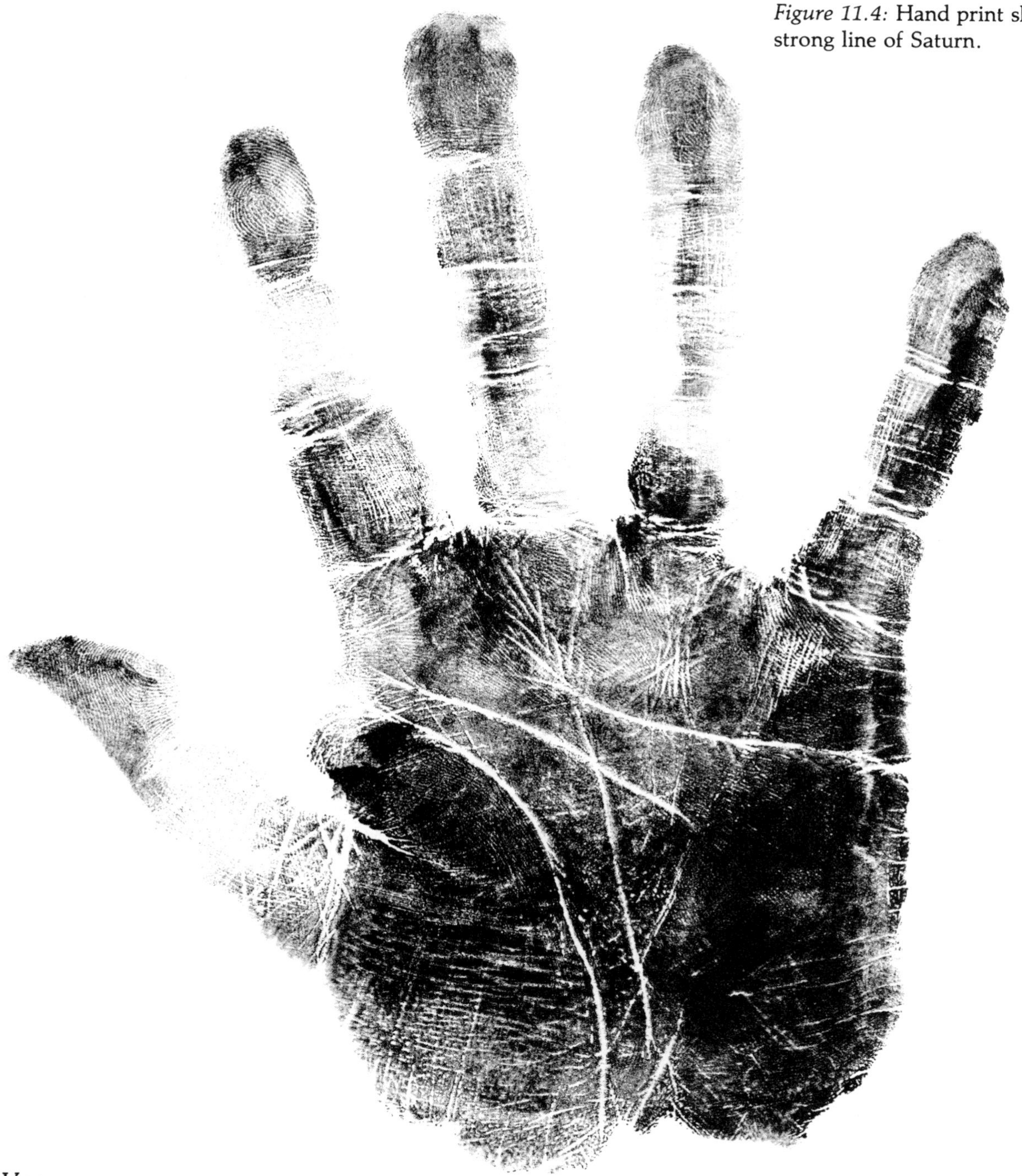

Figure 11.4: Hand print showing a strong line of Saturn.

Venus

The mount of Venus reflects our passion and capacity to love. While some people with a strong mount of Venus may laughingly reply 'sex therapist' when asked about their favourite career, few actual career choices are determined by this mount alone.

Nevertheless, a strong mount of Venus imparts love, sympathy and passion to the personality, and will add warmth, kindness and humanity to the power of the other mounts. Unlike a strong mount of Saturn, which favours isolation, a prominent mount of Venus encourages personal involvement and commitment. It will make the medical doctor more

129

Figure 11.5: Hand print showing Saturn line running together with the life line at its beginning.

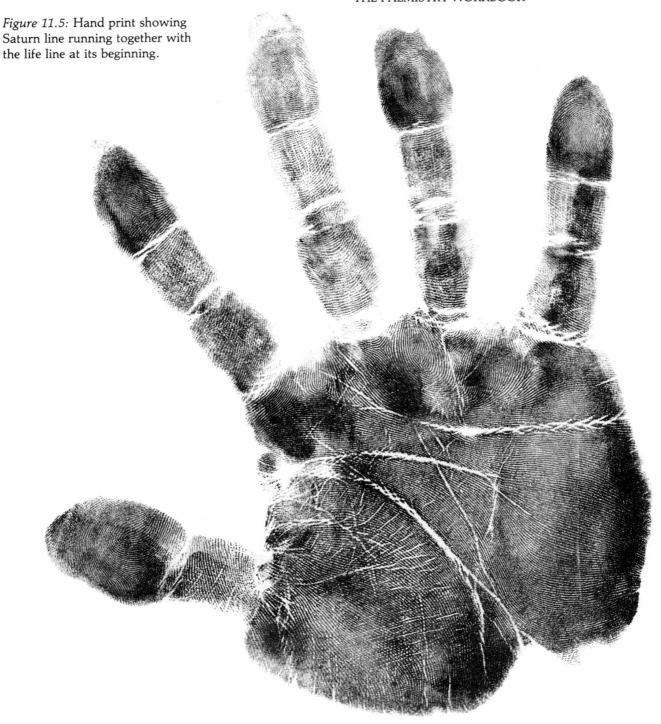

caring, a teacher more concerned, and an executive more likely to respond to human needs and priorities than to business advantages alone.

SATURN: THE LINE OF LIFE TASK

Although the mounts and fingers are important guides to career direction, the line of Saturn reveals how satisfied we are in our career and the degree

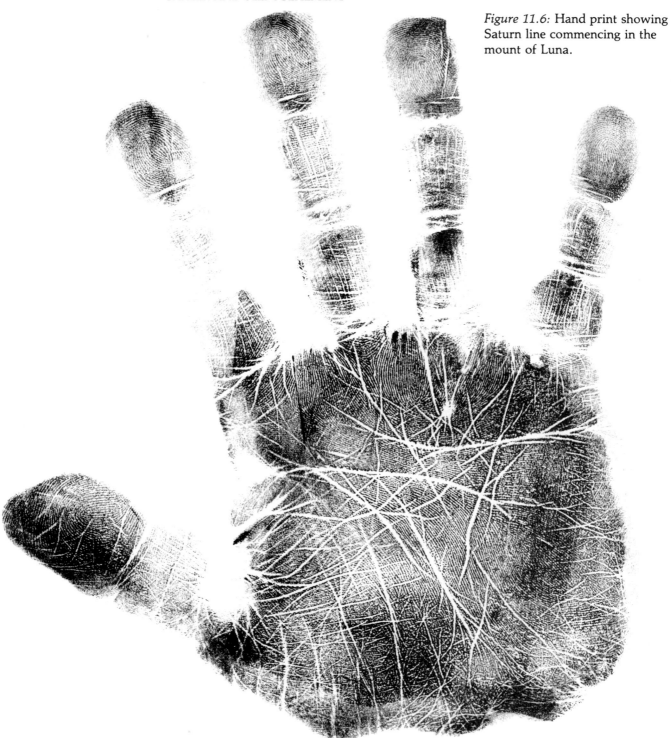

Figure 11.6: Hand print showing Saturn line commencing in the mount of Luna.

to which we are fulfilling our life task.

The stronger and clearer the line of Saturn, the more content we are with the direction of our life. If a wealthy executive is unhappy with his vocation, the line will probably be weak and fragmented, even if he is regarded as a success by others. By the same token, the man who shines the executive's shoes every morning and is happy with his work will probably possess a Saturn line that is strong and clearly marked.

131

Figure 11.7: Hand print showing poor Saturn line.

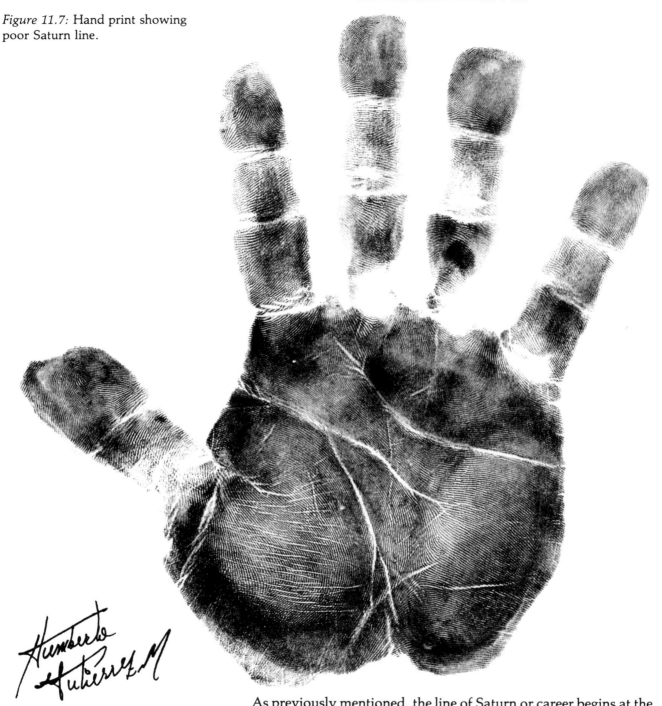

As previously mentioned, the line of Saturn or career begins at the base of the palm between the mounts of Venus and Luna, and moves upwards towards the Saturn finger, as seen in Figure 11.4. This would indicate that the individual — in this instance an internationally acclaimed opera singer — knew her life path since she was a teenager and began to pursue her career at that time. The Saturn line continues to be strong until the age of fifty, when it reveals a movement into several different areas of interest.

In general, the later the Saturn line begins on the hand, the later in life the person will find their true vocation.

132

When the Saturn line runs together with the life line at its commencement (Figure 11.5) it is often difficult to establish oneself in a career. This may be primarily due to pressure or expectation from parents. When the Saturn line begins inside the life line, the influence of the parents is especially strong.

When the line begins in the mount of Luna (Figure 11.6) the person's life path will probably be extremely varied, with a potential for several careers and frequent relocations. When the Saturn line continues deep into the mount of Saturn (also seen in Figure 11.6) the person will probably remain active past retirement age. This print is that of an agronomist, who served in the Peace Corps upon his retirement. Before his death at the age of eighty two, he continued to be actively involved in theosophy, his masonic lodge, and his church, as seen by the three small branches at the end of the Saturn line.

When the Saturn line ends deep in the mount of Jupiter, the career involves leadership or work in the public eye.

When the line ends between the mounts of Saturn and Apollo, the career may be related to some aspect of the arts, or can be an indication of money or fame.

The presence of a good line of Apollo tends to strengthen the Saturn line. An additional verticle line running near the Saturn line may indicate an additional career or avocational interest. In the print of the agronomist (Figure 11.6) the short line — which eventually crosses the Saturn line a centimetre above the heart line — may indicate his several years of university teaching.

If the career line is strong and deep, the person will realize the potential the line offers. A strong line also reveals confidence, determination and satisfaction in work.

If this line is thin, shallow or absent (Figure 11.7) there is often a struggle to fulfil one's career ambitions. Frustration and lack of focus in life are common.

Islands on the Saturn line reveal a need for greater focus of both energy and ideas. Obstacles to the career are often indicated.

Breaks on this line reveal periods of transition and possible lack of career direction.

A wavy Saturn line is a sign of irregular endurance in one's chosen career or direction. The person tends to be more of a 'Jack of all trades' as opposed to a specialist in one or two fields.

Branches moving upward from this line add strength to the line at the age they appear, while downward branches indicate career disappointments.

When we look at the hand in relation to career and life task, we must remember that *no one is a victim of the universe* and that we create our own reality. Each of us has a specific task or tasks in life and a goal to accomplish.

Understanding the message of the hand can guide us towards becoming aware of our hidden talents and aspirations, and can help us bridge the gap between our inner desires and outer reality. By taking responsibility for our life path, we can come into contact with what we *really* want on a deep level. The result is greater happiness, joy and inner peace.

SECTION IV:
PRACTICAL HAND
ANALYSIS

By this time you should have a thorough conceptual grounding in the essence of hand analysis. In the following chapters we will examine the more practical 'how-to' aspects of reading hands and taking hand prints.

Chapter 12

HOW TO READ HANDS

Reading the hand of another is a very serious matter, involving tremendous responsibility. Simply stated, hand analysis involves one person letting another person study a part of his or her body and then make pronouncements on highly personal and sensitive issues. In a sense, hand analysis can be compared to reading someone's private letters or journals. For this reason, a hand reader must bear responsibility for both what is said and how it is expressed during a consultation.

The underlying intent of the hand reader is of primary importance. Hand analysis must never be used to impress or seduce, or to gain power or control over another's life. Efforts must be made to be as objective as possible, while maintaining close contact with the other person during the reading. Honesty is an essential component of each hand analysis, yet we must phrase every observation and suggestion in a way that is truthful, kind and non-judgemental. If what we have to say does not satisfy these three requirements, it is better to say nothing.

At the same time, we need to avoid the tendency to focus only on the positive aspects of the hand. While we should help the individual become aware of his talents and abilities, we do him no favour by glossing over negative aspects or areas of conflict in his life.

Closely related to this issue is *timing*. In certain situations it is not appropriate to reveal information, especially if we feel that it would cause unnecessary pain or if the person would not be able to deal with the particular issue or problem.

Although our primary goal should be to help those who come to us for a consultation, it is important to realize that, as hand readers, we are not practising therapy. Therapy involves a regular, ongoing process in the deep psychological change of the individual which should only be performed by a qualified psychotherapist. Counselling, on the other hand, is relatively brief and is usually intended to work with specific areas of concern, such as health, career or relationship. Although a hand reader's task often involves some level of counselling, it is not our major goal. Rather, our primary task is that of *education*, involving a one-time consultation consisting of the simple sharing of information. The person receiving the reading wants to be told about him or herself with the goal of expanding self-knowledge and personal well-being. While it is often possible that a consultation may lead the individual to seek counselling or therapy, this is not the reader's main task. For this reason, many chirologists discourage frequent consultations (usually limiting them to one or two a year) while referring the 'client' to an appropriate counsellor, therapist or health professional as needed.

Perhaps one of the most difficult lessons for the hand reader is to take a personal interest in the client while remembering that the client is responsible for his or her own life. Nevertheless, when major life issues are exposed and discussed, we should never leave the client hanging, but should try to lead him or her to the 'next step' whenever possible. According to Stephen Arroyo in his excellent book *Astrology, Psychology and the Four Elements*:

> One should realize that merely giving advice without also giving a means for deeper understanding is of little value, for each person must do his or her own work and must, through his or her own experience, arrive at the higher awareness that enables the person to outgrow or transcend the difficulty.

In addition to possible referral to a counsellor or therapist, such a process may involve eliciting reactions and questions, so that the client will take a more active role in the reading rather than being merely a passive listener. This participation also leads to their seeking solutions to problems by themselves. Very often we know the solutions to our problems on a deep level, but are accustomed to avoiding them or having someone else provide the solution.

Respect for privacy is often overlooked by hand readers. In my own work, I prefer to read an individual's hands alone, in a quiet setting, without the involvement of a third party looking on and asking questions. Although the presence of a tape recorder tends to encourage the client to pay less attention to the reading as it is being given, I don't object to its use. I never discuss a reading with others; at the time I read someone's hand, it is *our* business, but after the consultation is over, the information discussed is no longer my affair.

TECHNIQUE

There is no one method or technique to reading a hand. Although I encourage each reader to develop a method which works best for him or her, the following general procedure may be helpful.

Preparation

Before you are to read another's hand, try to become aware of both the privilege and the responsibility involved. Meditation and prayer are useful to help you get grounded in your 'core' or higher self, and to come into closer contact with your intuition.

Before you look at the person's hands, ask if he or she has ever had a reading before. Point out that the hands show tendencies and not always definite facts, and that the lines of the hand can change within a matter of weeks. I often mention as an aside that I know of some very old people with short life lines, as well as young people with long life lines who have been killed in accidents.

Ask the person's age and find out if they are right or left handed. Explain that the passive hand is more the storehouse of our potential while the active hand more clearly expresses what we are doing with it.

Looking at the hands

Sitting directly across from the client, take both hands in yours and look at them. Close your eyes for a moment and say a silent prayer to help you focus and do your best. I prefer a simple 'Thy will be done' while a friend prefers 'I pray that all I may now tell him/her will be for his/her highest good and for the highest good of all concerned'. This momentary spiritual focusing need not be so obvious as to be noticed by the person you are reading for, but can appear as though you are merely collecting your thoughts before proceeding with the reading.

Look carefully at both hands. Take note of the size, shape, skin texture and flexibility. Note the positions and length of the fingers, taking account of the basic hand types. Don't be afraid to touch, bend, and squeeze the hand gently as you examine it.

Observe the fingers carefully, taking special note of their size, flexibility, shape and contour. Are any of the fingers bent? Which are prominent and which are weak? How are they held on the hand?

Turn the hands over and observe the nails, and ask the person to open the hands wide. Check out the knuckles as well as the relative position of the fingers to each other and to the hand as a whole.

Turn the hand over again and examine the mounts. Run your finger over each mount and judge their relative strength. Note any special markings on the mounts, such as squares, crosses and grilles.

Look at the lines, taking careful notice of their strength, clarity and length. Where do they begin and where do they end? Are there breaks, dots or islands on the lines? Are there branches or colour changes? How do the lines differ on each hand?

After examining the hands for a few minutes, you will get a 'feel' for the hand and a basic understanding of who the person is you are reading. At this point, take the active hand and begin reading, being ready to look to the passive hand for confirming or contrasting traits. Begin the reading at a point which feels most appropriate. With some people you may decide immediately to discuss health issues, while with others you might begin with some observations about character or career. Use your judgement.

Continue your reading, being sure to cover all areas of interest including health, life history, intelligence, emotional characteristics, career, travel, relationships, and other aspects like creativity and spirituality. Proceed slowly, always being open to intuitive messages from your subconscious. Make frequent eye contact with the client. You may prefer to answer questions during the reading, or ask for questions when you are done.

Throughout the reading, try to keep the following issues in the back of your mind and ask yourself if you are dealing with them:

- What is the person really looking for?
- What is he/she ready to hear?
- Is what I am saying appropriate for the person at this time?
- What is the best approach to help this person develop his/her sense of initiative, responsibility and participation in life?
- Does this reading touch on sensitive issues of my own which may affect the reading and my objectivity?
- Am I making myself clear and am I being understood?

At the conclusion of the reading, people often ask questions like 'Will I get married (or divorced)?', 'How many children will I have?' and the classic 'When am I going to die?'. Since the hands show probabilities and therefore can change, make it clear that any specific prediction is pure guesswork. As we mentioned earlier in the text, *never* predict the time of death.

When practised with care, sensitivity and humility, hand analysis can be an endless source of adventure, learning and inspiration. By helping others increase their self-knowledge, we invariably deepen our own. By helping others 'remove the stones from the path' we open our own channel of compassion and service.

Chapter 13

HOW TO TAKE HAND PRINTS

One of the best ways to deepen our understanding of the hand is to maintain a record of the hands we analyze. Although plaster casts of hands faithfully show the form and lines, they are complicated to make and extremely difficult to store. Photographs of the hands are simpler to make and are easier to store, but often involve considerable expense.

The easiest and cheapest method of recording hands is the taking of palm prints. Although the prints do not always reveal the exact hand shape, lines and skin ridges can be — with practice — faithfully reproduced. When used in conjunction with the Hand Analysis Test Chart described later on, a collection of hand prints can be very useful. In addition to providing a permanent record of the hand itself, subsequent follow-up prints can reveal changes in the hand over the years.

Materials

The materials necessary for taking hand prints are both inexpensive and easy to obtain:

1. A rubber roller approximately four inches (10cm) wide.
2. A tube of black water-base block printing (lino) ink.
3. Good quality art paper. You may prefer single sheets, or a spiral-bound art book for easier storage.
4. A thin pad of foam rubber to provide a suitable cushion for the paper.
5. A sheet of glass, linoleum or newspaper for applying the ink.

Procedure

First, you lay the paper over the foam rubber, which helps mould the paper to conform to the contours of the hand. Roll out the ink on the glass, linoleum or newspaper. (Figure 13.1)

Carefully ink the subject's hand, using just enough ink to lightly cover the entire palmar surface (Figure 13.2)

Have the subject place their hand on the paper in a natural way. Apply pressure to the entire hand (paying special attention to the centre of the palm and the space between the finger mounts) in order to obtain a complete impression. (Figure 13.3)

Hold the paper to the table as the hand is slowly withdrawn. This will prevent the print from blurring. (Figure 13.4)

Figure 13.1

Figure 13.2

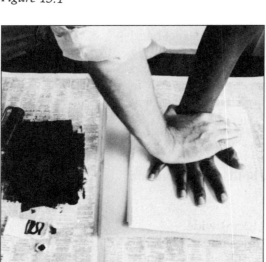

Figure 13.3

Figure 13.4

In addition to the print itself, you should include a record of the major features of the hand, such as the shape, dominant fingers and mounts, as well as personal data concerning the individual whose print you are including in your collection. A suggested Hand Analysis Test Chart is included here for your convenience.

HAND ANALYSIS TEST CHART

Name:
Date of birth:
Today's date:

Predominant hand type:
Strongest mounts
Weakest mounts

Tests:
Skin texture
Skin colour
Flexibility
Consistency

Fingers (describe):
Jupiter
Saturn
Apollo
Mercury
Predominant
Longer or shorter than palm
Straight
Bent

Thumb:
Size
Flexibility
How set (low, medium, high)
Will phalange (describe)
Logic phalange (describe)

Nails:
Size
Shape
Colour
Unusual features

Additional comments/personal data

Chapter 14

ANALYSIS OF HAND PRINTS

A number of interesting prints from the author's collection follow. Each is accompanied by a brief 'thumbnail' description.

Analysis 1 (Figure 14.1)
The hand of Aaron Copland, the renowned American composer and conductor. Note the long, clear and gently sloping head line, indicating high intelligence and a strong abstract mind. The small lines moving up a prominent mount of Luna show that intuition and instinct play a major role in the maestro's compositions. Of special interest are the unusually strong and clear line of Apollo (creative brilliance, accomplishment and fame) and the long Apollo and Mercury fingers, indicating a strong ability to communicate.

Analysis 2 (Figure 14.2)
The hand of a thirty-six-year-old woman. She is the director of several corporations, including one of the most prestigious architecture and design firms in France. The broadness of the palm coupled with short fingers show that many of her business decisions are based on instinct. The career line is strong and clear, as is the Apollo line, revealing achievement and financial rewards. Her head line is more realistic than imaginative, and the strong thumb provides both strength and determination. In addition to her career, the subject is a licensed helicopter pilot and travels an average of 50,000 miles a year for business and pleasure.

Analysis 3 (Figure 14.3)
The hand of a twenty-four-year-old dancer. A former member of the Martha Graham Dance Company, he later founded his own company along with his wife, who is also an accomplished dancer. The overall statement of the hand is one of strength and balance. The life line is reinforced by several inner life lines, increasing energy and strengthening the constitution. The heart line is sensitive though not over-long, and is accompanied by a rare near-perfect girdle of Venus. These strong emotions are balanced by a long head line, curving upwards at the end, which is said to indicate strong athletic ability. His prominent low-set thumb reveals a strong will. The career line was just beginning to take form at the age this print was taken.

Figure 14.1: Hand print of Aaron Copland, composer and conductor.

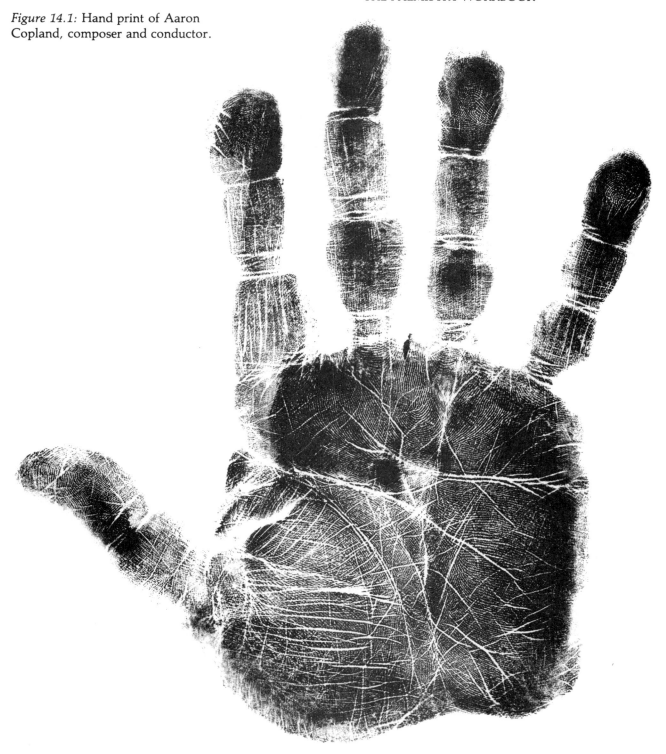

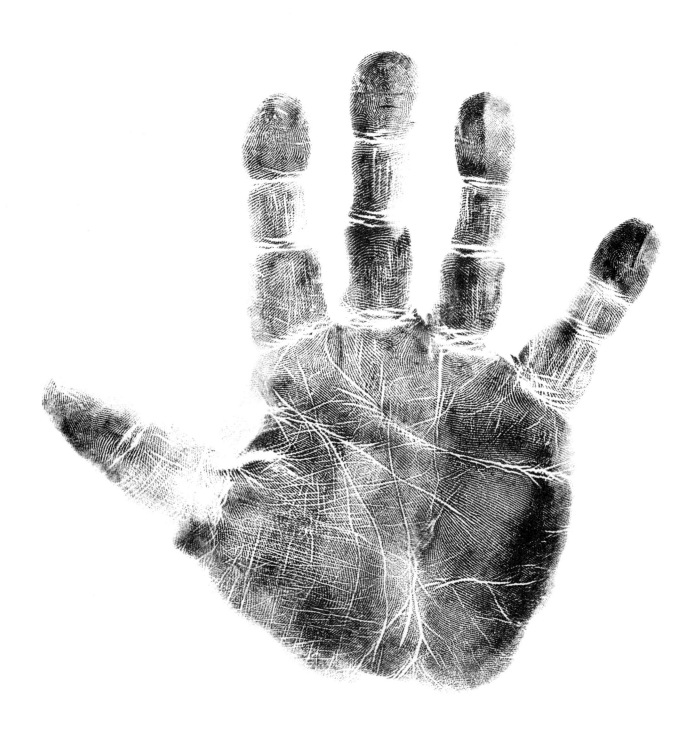

Figure 14.2: Hand print of successful businesswoman.

Figure 14.3: Hand print of young male dancer.

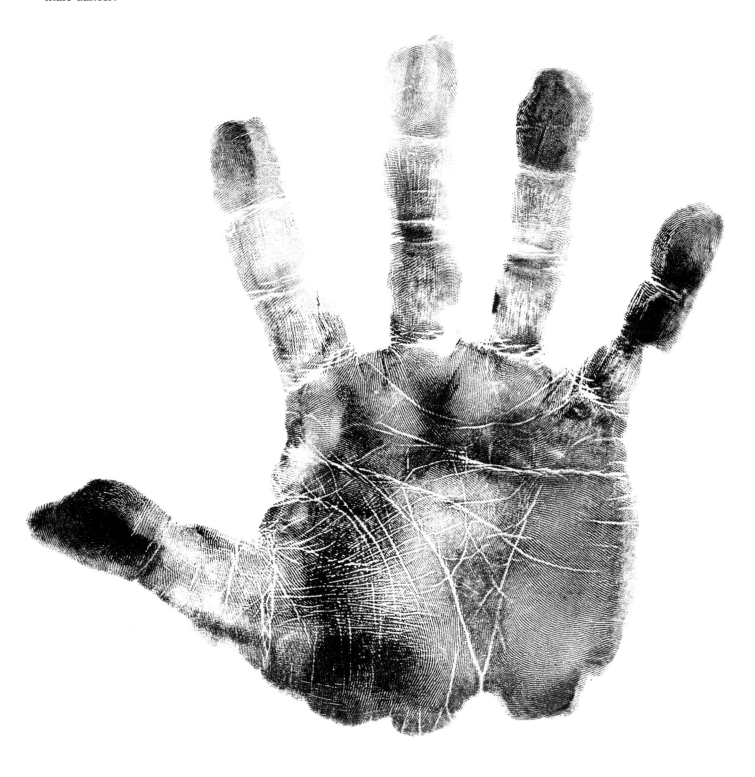

Figure 14.4: Hand print of four-year-old girl.

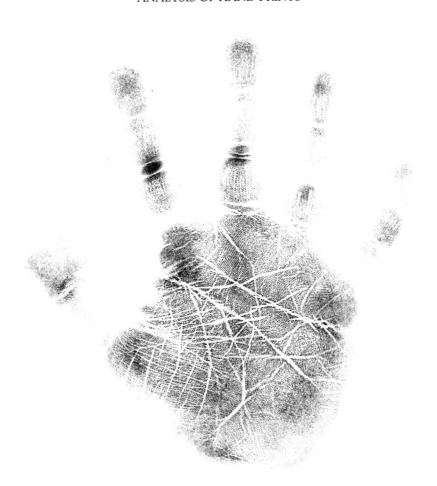

Analysis 4 (Figure 14.4)

The hand of a four-year-old-girl. Even at an early age the personality is clearly defined. The strong head line reveals intelligence, and the prominent thumb shows stubbornness and determination. The life line is clear, though not especially strong; the line of Saturn — at least in part — 'covers' the life line and adds to its strength. Later on, the Saturn line forms a branch and eventually moves (after a break between the heart and head lines) towards the Jupiter finger, indicating a possible career involving leadership or politics. The fact that the strong Jupiter finger stands apart from the other fingers would reinforce this possibility.

Analysis 5 (Figures 14.5 and 14.6)

These are prints of thirty-four-year-old twins, born eight minutes apart. Although the brothers are identical in outward appearance, their hands reveal numerous differences regarding personality and career.

Reinaldo (Figure 14.5) is an accomplished architect. Although his heart line predominates, the head line becomes stronger and better defined after the age of twenty-seven or twenty-eight. His strong imagination and intuition play an important role in his innovative architectural designs. The strong line of Apollo (although obscure in the print) reveals achievement and creative ability.

Figure 14.5: Hand print of an architect.

Humberto (Figure 14.6) is a successful lawyer. Like his twin, Humberto's heart line is very long and deep, indicating that he is primarily guided by his feelings. His hand contains more lines than the hand of his brother, which would indicate that he is more nervous and highly strung. In addition, his life line is not as strong as Reinaldo's, which would indicate less resistance to disease, probably due to stress-related factors. Although the head line slopes downwards, it is more 'practical' than that of his twin, which would probably make him better suited for a career

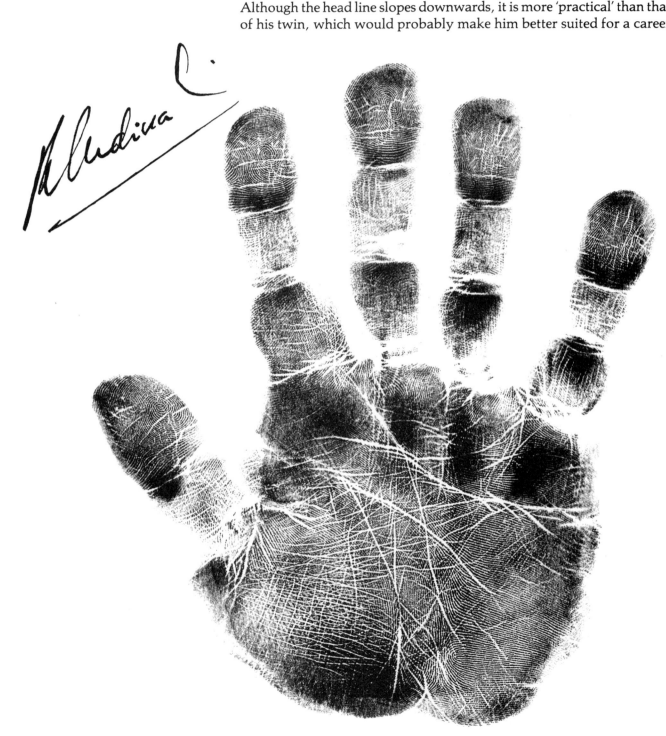

in law. Unlike his brother, Humberto is extremely psychic (as seen by the strong lines moving up the Luna mount) and is involved in spiritual healing, as indicated by the tiny Samaritan lines on the mount of Mercury.

Figure 14.6: Hand print of a lawyer, twin brother to the architect of Figure 14.5.

Analysis 6 (Figure 14.7)
The energy and strength in these lines are tremendous. The hand belongs to a thirty-three-year-old man who works as a financial consultant to theatre companies and other cultural organizations. In addition to

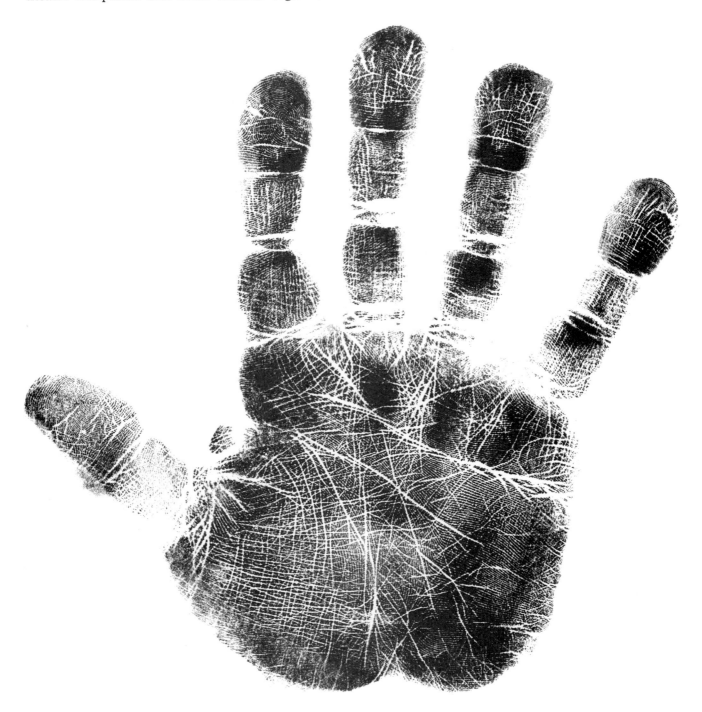

Figure 14.7: Hand print of a busy
financial consultant.

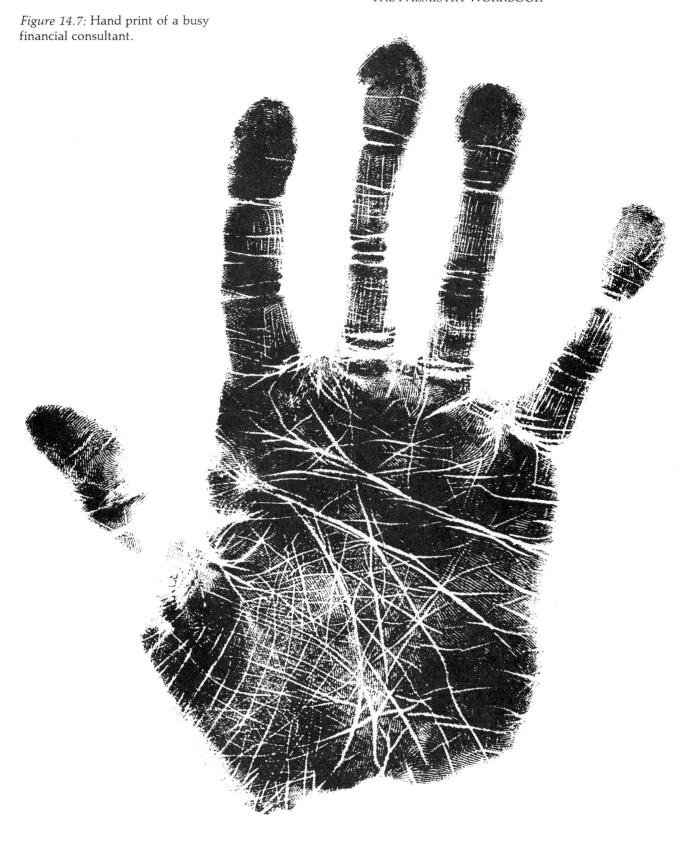

devoting his energies toward dance, bodybuilding and gymnastics, the subject has a deep spiritual nature and meditates for more than an hour per day.

The major lines are long and deep. However, the rare overlapping double head lines are worthy of special note. The upper line (which branches at the end) reveals a realistic and practical way of perceiving the world, while the lower head line indicates a strong imagination. Together, they form a clear intellect which is balanced and decisive. The subject is a member of MENSA, an organization open only to those with an exceptionally high IQ.

Several modifying factors are also present. The connecting lines of head and life tend to decrease spontaneity and self-reliance, while the short Jupiter finger indicates low self-esteem. The high-set thumb also tends to hold him back from fully utilizing his considerable talents.

BIBLIOGRAPHY

Aristotle, *Chiromantia*, (Ulm: Johann Reger, 1490).

d'Arpentigny, Stanislaus, *La chirognomie, ou l'art de reconnaître les tendances de l'intelligence d'après les formes de la main* (Paris: Charles Le Clere, 1843).

Arroyo, Stephen, *Astrology, Psychology and the Four Elements* (Davis, California: CRCS Publications, 1975).

Ayer, V. A. K., *Sariraka Shastra* (Bombay: D. B. Taraporevala, 1960).

Bacher, Elman, *Studies in Astrology*, Vols. 1 and 2 (Oceanside, California: The Rosicrucian Fellowship, 1962).

Banerji, Sudhakar, *Palmistry, Sex and Marriage* (New Delhi: Sagar Publications, 1962).

Benham, William G., *How to Choose Vocations from the Hand* (New Delhi: Sagar Publications, 1967).

Benham, William G., *The Laws of Scientific Hand Reading* (New York: Putnam and Co., 1958).

Brenner, Elizabeth, *The Hand Book* (Millbrae, California: Celestial Arts, 1980).

Buhler, G., trans., *The Laws of Manu* (New York: Dover Publications Inc., 1969).

Colomar, Orencia, *Quirología* (Barcelona: Plaza and Janes, 1973).

Fairchild, Dennis, *The Handbook of Humanistic Palmistry* (Ferndale, Michigan: Thumbs Up! Publications, 1980).

Fitzherbert, Andrew, *Hand Analysis* (New South Wales; Angus & Robertson, 1986).

Gaafar, M. M., *Ilm-ul-Kaff* (Bombay: D. B. Taraporevala, 1964).

Gettings, Fred, *The Book of the Hand* (London: Paul Hamlyn, 1965).

Giles, Herbert A., 'Palmistry in China' in *The Nineteenth Century and After*, December 1904.

Hartleib, Johann, *Die Kunst Chiromantia* (Germany: 1475).

Hutchinson, Beryl, *Your Life in Your Hands* (London: Sphere 1969).

Issberner-Haldane, Ernest, *El diagnóstico por la mano y el diagnóstico por la una* (Buenos Aires: Editorial Kier, 1966).

Issberner-Haldane, Ernest, *Tratado de quirosofía (Die Wissenschaftliche Handlesekunst Chirosophie)* (Buenos Aires: Editorial Kier, 1966).

Jaquin, Noel, *The Hand of Man* (London: Faber and Faber Ltd., 1933).

Jaquin, Noel, *The Signature of Time* (London: Faber and Faber Ltd., 1950).

Krumm-Heller, Arnold, *Tratado de quirología médica* (Buenos Aires: Editorial Kier, 1964).

Lanza, Gloria A., *The Concept of the Spiritual Aspect of Man with Implications for Counselors*. Thesis, Hunter College, New York, June, 1979.

MacKenzie, Nancy, *Palmistry for Women* (New York: Warner Books Inc., 1973).

Pierrakos, John C., *Creative Aspects of the Ego in the Core Energetic Process* (New York: Institute for the New Age, 1977).

Révész, Gésa, *The Human Hand* (London: Routledge and Kegan Paul, 1958).

Rosenblum, Bernard, *The Astrologer's Guide to Counselling* (Reno, Nevada: CRCS Publications, 1983).

Scheimann, Eugene, *A Doctor's Guide to Better Health Through Palmistry* (West Nyack, New York: Parker Publishing Co. Inc., 1969).

Sen, K. C., *Hast Samudrika Shastra* (Bombay: D. B. Taraporevala, 1960).

Sorell, Walter, *The Story of the Human Hand* (Indianapolis: The Bobbs-Merrill Co., 1967).

Spier, Julius, *The Hands of Children* (London: Routledge and Kegan Paul Ltd., 1955).

Steinbach, Martin, *Medical Palmistry* (Secaucus, New Jersey: University Books, 1975).

Wolff, Charlotte, *The Human Hand* (New York: Alfred A. Knopf, 1943).

Wolff, Charlotte, *The Hand in Psychological Diagnosis* (London: Methuen and Co. Ltd., 1951).

INDEX